DEAD
In Their Tracks

Stopping the Liberal / Skeptic Attack on the Bible

by

John Noē
Author of
Beyond the End Times
Shattering the 'Left Behind' Delusion
The Apocalypse Conspiracy

This material was originally presented and read as a theological paper at the 45th Meeting of the Midwestern Region of the Evangelical Theological Society, March 2000, in Florissant, Missouri, at Saint Louis Christian College.

Micah L. Young

International Preterist Association
122 Seaward Avenue
Bradford, PA 16701-1515 USA

Library of Congress Cataloging-in-Publication Data
(In Application)
Noé, John, 1945-
  Dead In Their Tracks
1st edition
ISBN 0-9621311-5-6

Graphics By:
OmniGraphix Corporation
1-941-466-6220
www.omnigraphix.com

Dedication

*To current and future
seminary students,
pastors, and lay activists
who will engage the battle
and retake lost ground*

Cover Art

THE COVER ART OF DAVID AND GOLIATH IS ONE OF THE MANY BIBLICAL SCENES PAINTED BY MICHELANGELO ON THE CEILING OF THE SISTINE CHAPEL IN THE VATICAN.

Contents

Publisher's Preface: I Was There...by Edward E. Stevens vii

1 **Tracks of the Attack 1**

2 **When Did Jesus Say He Would Return 9**

3 **Side-Stepping Devices 13**

4 **Taking It Seriously 17**

5 **The Only Solution to the Problem of
   "Nonoccurrence" 21**

6 **Differing Opinions About Preterism 25**

7 **The Case for Occurrence—A Brief Overview 29**

8 **Daniel's "Time of the End" 39**

9 **Christ's Coming on the Clouds— a Long
   Biblical Precedent 43**

10 **In the Same Way, for the Same Purpose 49**

11   Why Does It Really Matter 55

Conclusion: Will You Join Us? 59

Publisher's Postscript:
Four Classic Objections **61**

Appendix A: *Your Worldview* **73**

Appendix B: *Futurism—*
        An Eschatology of Despair **79**

***Works Cited* 86**

Publisher's Preface

I Was There...

I was there when John Noē first presented some of the material contained in this book. The occasion was the 45th Meeting of the Midwestern Region of the Evangelical Theological Society. John read a paper entitled *The Only Solution to the Liberal/Skeptic Attack on the Bible.*

The room was packed with theologians, pastors, and scholars. John's presentation generated lots of questions and created quite a buzz in the hallways afterwards. Over the next two days, numerous folks came by our exhibit booth to learn more, or to discuss and debate it.

One Christian college instructor who had not attended John's lecture came by our exhibit booth and expressed his skepticism about the preterist view. John handed him a copy of *The Only Solution*...He took it, somewhat casually, and walked away. But when the very next session was over, he came bouncing back to our booth, announcing, "I'm convinced!"

"Convinced about what?" John asked.

"The preterist view," he replied.

"What changed you?" John queried.

"Your paper!" the instructor answered. He was holding it up—he had read it during the lecture session. "I need to know more about this," he added. "What other books can I read?"

It is not every day of the week that someone adopts preterism so quickly. It takes a powerful and compelling presentation to change minds that rapidly. This is that kind of book.

Noē's earlier ETS presentation called *The Only Solution...* has been given a new title, *Dead in Their Tracks*, and one of its arguments made even more compelling. Also, a Publisher's Preface and Postscript have been added. As a result, I believe this little book is a reformational message that all theologians, pastors, scholars, and Christians in the church today need to read and seriously contemplate, for these three reasons.

First, this book is a forceful response to the liberal/skeptic attack on the inspiration of the New Testament and the integrity of Christ. These critical scholars constantly taunt conservatives with the timeframe references, and we have failed to "answer them convincingly" (says R.C. Sproul)—until now! Nothing answers their charges of "nonoccurrence" and "non-fulfillment" better than the preterist view of "actual occurrence" and "real fulfillment." It is the only possible solution. While it does not address or answer all the arguments that the liberals and skeptics have posed, it does answer the big one they have incessantly used. And when the big one is answered, the rest of their arguments fall away.

Secondly, I appreciate very much the absolutely essential work that modern-day apologists are doing for the cause of Christ. Men such as R.C. Sproul, D. James Kennedy, Chuck Colson, Hank Hannegraaff, Gary DeMar, Ken Gentry, and many others are daily defending the faith against all kinds of attacks. These men are aware of the preterist view and have discovered some of its enormous apologetic power. But their partial preterist approach will not hold up against the liberal/skeptical onslaught. Only a completely consistent preterist approach can stop the liberals and the skeptics dead in their tracks. It is the little stone in the slingshot that can topple the whole Goliath complex that has dared mock the integrity of God, his inerrant Word, and Christ. Consequently, the

Preterist is not an enemy, but a fellow conservative in the battle against the liberal and skeptic. This book explains how the preterist view can unite us in our defense of the faith and give us a weapon our mutual enemies cannot withstand.

Thirdly, this book not only seeks to answer the critic and unite conservative apologists, but to recruit young conservative evangelical scholars who will help us take the fight back to liberal seminaries, denominations, colleges, theological journals and conferences, and recapture those institutions for truth. Our aim is to equip and train an army of young preterist reformers (before the liberals get them) who will cleanse the theological temples and restore confidence in God's inerrant Word. May this book be used by God to encourage them to take back the turf that the Philistines have plundered from us, and restore the Word of God to its rightful place at the center of our culture.

John Noē is a conservative evangelical scholar and a reformer. His passion is to inspire such a radical reform of the Church's eschatological views that all generations to come will be constructively influenced by it. I share his vision and passion.

This book is a loud wakeup call to a slumbering Church that has all but lost its will to counterattack. Read this and then passionately join us in this vision to unite fellow apologists and recruit the next generation to stop the liberals and skeptics dead in their tracks.

Edward E. Stevens
Publisher & President
International Preterist Association

Chapter 1

Tracks of the Attack

In America over the past 50 to 100 years, seminary after seminary, church after church, and believer after believer have fallen victim to the liberal/skeptic attack on the Bible. They have departed from the conservative faith. It's called the "battle for the Bible." How or why has this happened? Critics have hit Christianity at its weakest point. Read it for yourself:

- Atheist **Bertrand Russell**, in his book *Why I Am Not A Christian*, discredits the inspiration of the New Testament:

    I am concerned with Christ as He appears in the Gospels . . . there one does find some things that do not seem to be very wise. . . For one thing, He certainly thought that His second coming would occur in clouds of glory before the death of all the people who were living at the time. There are a great many texts that prove that. . . . He believed that His coming would happen during the lifetime of many then living. That was the belief of his earlier followers, and it was the basis of a good deal of his moral teaching.[1]

---

[1] Bertrand Russell, *Why I Am Not A Christian* (New York: A Touchtone Book by Simon & Schuster, 1957), 16.

Russell reasoned that it would be fallacious to follow a religious leader (such as Jesus) who was mistaken on so basic a prediction as his parousia.

- Liberal **Albert Schweitzer**, in his 19th-century book *The Quest of the Historical Jesus,* Schweitzer summarized the problem of "Parousia delay" as follows:

   The whole history of 'Christianity' down to the present day... is based on the delay of the Parousia, the nonoccurrence of the Parousia, the abandonment of eschatology, the process and completion of the 'de-eschatologizing' of religion which has been connected therewith.[2]

- **Jewish skeptics** contend that Jesus didn't complete the whole mission of the Messiah within the time frame their prophets had predicted. They allege that Christians invented the idea of a "second coming" off in the future to cover up Jesus' failure to return as He promised. This is the Jews' primary excuse for rejecting Jesus and belittling Christianity. Prominent orthodox rabbis and Jewish scholars have written:

   The main task of the Messiah was to bring the world back to G-d, and to abolish all war, suffering and injustice from the world. Clearly, Jesus did not accomplish this. In order to get around this failure on the part of Jesus, Christians invented the doctrine of the "Second Coming.". . . All the prophecies that Jesus did not fulfill the first time are supposed to be taken care of the second time around. However, the Jewish Bible

---

[2] Albert Schweiterzer, *The Quest of the Historical Jesus* (New York: The Macmillan Company, eighth printing, 1973), 360.

offers absolutely no evidence to support the Christian doctrine of a "Second Coming."[3]

The idea of a second coming is a pure rationalization of Jesus' failure to function in any way as a messiah, or to fulfill any of the prophecies of the Torah or the Prophets. The idea is purely a Christian invention, with no foundation in the Bible.[4]

This two-fold misapprehension of Jesus—the nearness of the kingdom of heaven and his Messiahship—perpetuated his memory and created Christianity. Had not the disciples expected his second coming Christianity could never have come into being: even as a Jewish sect. . . . The Jews as a whole could not, however, follow after a belief based on so slight a foundation. . . . Yet again, through the preaching of his messianic claims, after he had failed to manifest himself to the world again, in his power and glory, he became, in spite of himself, a "sacrifice," a "ransom for many."[5]

The success of the Christian claim or its failure rests to a very large extent on the theory of the second coming. . . . The Jews never had the concept of a second coming, and since it was the Jews themselves who first taught the notion of a Messiah, via the Jewish prophets, it seems quite reasonable to respect their opinion more than anyone else's. . . . the theory of the second coming is not based on Jewish tradition or sources, and is a theory born from desperation.[6]

---

[3] Aryeh Kaplan (orthodox rabbi), "Jesus and the Bible," in *The Real Messiah* (reprinted from *Jewish Youth*, June 1973, Tammuz 5733, No. 40), 57.

[4] Pinchas Stolper (orthodox rabbi), "Was Jesus the Messiah Let's Examine the Facts," in *The Real Messiah* (reprinted from *Jewish Youth*, June 1973, Tammuz 5733, No. 40), 46-47.

[5] Joseph Klausner (scholar), *Jesus of Nazareth: His Life, Times, and Teaching* (New York: Macmillen, 1925), 405.

[6] Samuel Levine (educator and debater). *You Take Jesus, I'll Take God: How To Refute Christian Missionaries* (Los Angeles: Hamoroh Press, 1980), 15, 23, 49.

- **Muslim skeptics** paint Christianity as a failed and false religion. They acknowledge that Jesus was a prophet, but discredit his divinity and destroy the credibility of the Bible by pointing out alleged errors and inconsistencies concerning his *perceived* non-return (among other things). They rightly recognize the logical implications of the Bible's time statements as having a direct bearing on the messianic and divine claims of Christ. In spite of this, "Muslims have great respect and love for Jesus. . . . He is one of the greatest prophets of Allah."[7] Therefore, they believe that either Jesus never spoke any time-restricting words concerning his return or the Apostles lied about his imminent return, and other eschatological matters, and corrupted the New Testament by adding words to this effect. These arguments naturally seek to undermine the inspiration and inerrancy of the Bible and open the door for the acceptance of the Qur'an and Islam—the fastest growing religion in the world, the second largest in the world, and soon, if not already by some estimates, the second largest in America.[8]

One of many Muslim web sites expresses their view thusly:

> We will instead present the following verses with regard to WHEN Jesus' second coming is supposed to occur. They are self explanatory but this has not prevented some [Christians] from inventing new abstract meanings for them:
> - ". . ." Matthew 24:29-34. How many generations have passed since?

---

[7] Badru D. Kateregga, *Islam and Christianity: A Muslim and a Christian in Dialogue* (Grand Rapids: Eerdmans, 1980, *re. ed* 1981), 131.

[8] Robert A. Morey, *The Islamic Invasion: Confronting the World's Fastest Growing Religion* (Eugene, Or.: Harvest House, 1992). Wendy Murry Zoba, "Islam, U.S.A.: Are Christians Prepared for Muslims in the Mainstream?," *Christianity Today Magazize*, 3 April 2000, 40.

- "..." Mark 13:23-30. How many generations have passed now?
- "..." Matthew 10:22-23. They have not only gone over all the cities of Israel, but have dispersed throughout all of the Earth and we are still waiting.
- "..." Matthew 16:27-28. Are there any of those who were standing who are alive to this day? Is this not further proof of mankind's tendency to put words in the mouth of Jesus (pbuh) which he never said?

At first, the Christian community expected an imminent return of Christ. . . . This hope carried on in the second century. When the second coming failed to occur, the church organized itself as a permanent institution under the leadership of its bishops. This, however, did not stop the predictions of "the second coming" . . . . Muslims too believe in the second coming of Jesus (pbuh). However, Muslims are told that Jesus (pbuh) was not forsaken by God to the Jews to be killed, rather, he was raised by God and it was made to appear to those present that he was crucified (Jesus' apostle Barnabas tells us that it was Judas the traitor who was taken to be crucified) [see Qur'an 4:155-157]. Muslims are also told that he will not return to earth until just before the end of time, and not that he will return before the death of his own generation, as stated above.[9]

Paradoxically, the view most prevalent in Christian evangelical circles regarding the timing of Christ's supposed "second coming" is more aligned with this Muslim statement/view than with the numerous biblical references to Jesus' return being within the lifetime of his contemporaries.

---

[9] Answering-Christianity.com, "The Ultimate Test of Jesus: Jesus' second coming and 'grace,'" (accessed 20 March 2000); available from http://www.arabianebarzaar.com/ac/second.htm; Internet.

Likewise, most Christians are unaware that the Bible never mentions an "end of time."

For these reasons and more, Muslims believe that the current Bible is not all of the true word of God and has been corrupted. The Qur'an along with other Islamic sacred texts are more accurate testaments, make more sense, and are absent of contradictions:

> The accusation that Jews and Christians had falsified their Scriptures... is the most basic Muslim argument against both the Old and New Testaments....In the Qur'an it is a central theme, used mainly to explain away the contradictions between the Bible and the Qur'an, and to establish that the coming of Muhammad and the rise of Islam had indeed been predicted in the uncorrupted "true" Bible.[10]

> The first generation of Christians were convinced that Jesus would shortly return in glory. Despite the fact that this did not happen in their lifetime, the belief that he would return for the final judgment lingered on and became enshrined in the creeds. Throughout the history of the Church this belief has been the subject of renewed speculation during times of social and political upheaval.... The Qur'an itself does not explicitly refer to Jesus' return but the classical commentators detected allusions to it in 4:159 and 43:61 and occasionally elsewhere.[11]

> In tradition, *Hadith*, the basic body of religious sources second to the Qur'an, Islam lives in the vivid expectation of Jesus' second coming, ushering in the realm of peace and justice at the end of time, in which Muhammad plays no part. At the end of time, Jesus will descend . . . to slay the

---

[10] Hava Lazarus-Yafeh, *Intertwined Worlds: Medieval Islam and Bible Criticism* (Princeton, NJ: Princeton University Press, 1992), 19-20.

[11] Neal Robinson, *Christ in Islam and Christianity* (Albany: State University of New York Press, 1991), 78.

Antichrist. He will go to Jerusalem, perform the prayer at dawn in Muslim fashion and rid the world of all unbelievers and their symbols. All peoples of the book will believe in him, forming only one community, Islam, and the reign of justice and complete peace will set in. The reign of Jesus, God's glorified servant, will last forty years, followed by the 'Hour', the end of the world on the day when God alone will sit in judgment at the universal resurrection.[12]

It is the prophetic role of Muhammad . . . to witness the truth of Christ's Second Coming, which alone can bring into being the "universal Messianic reconciliation" . . . of Jews, Christians, and Muslims.[13]

- Even **C.S. Lewis**, the respected Christian apologist and author, we are embarrassed to report, said in 1960:

  "Say what you like,' we shall be told [by the skeptic], "the apocalyptic beliefs of the first Christians have been proved to be false. It is clear from the New Testament that they all expected the Second Coming in their own lifetime. And, worse still, they had a reason, and one which you will find very embarrassing. Their Master had told them so. He shared, and indeed created, their delusion. He said in so many words, 'this generation shall not pass till all these things be done.' And He was wrong. He clearly knew no more about the end of the world than anyone else."

  It is certainly the most embarrassing verse in the Bible. Yet how teasing, also, that within fourteen words of it should come the statement "but of that day and that hour knoweth no man, no, not the angels which are in heaven, neither the Son,

---

[12] Hans Kung and Jurgen Moltmann, eds., *Islam: A Challenge for Christianity* (London: SCM Press, 1994), 108.
[13] Yvonne Yazbeck Haddad and Wadi Z. Haddah, eds., *Christian-Muslim Encounters* (Gainesville: University Press of Florida, 1995), 433.

but the Father." The one exhibition of error and the one confession of ignorance grow side by side.[14]

Do you *hear* what these critics and even C.S. Lewis are saying? They are saying Jesus was *literally wrong* when He made numerous time-restrictive predictions and statements regarding his coming, his return. As we shall see, the embarrassment belongs to C.S. Lewis, et al. But this perceived weakness was, and still is, the crack that let the liberals in the door to begin their systematic criticism and dismantling of Scripture with its inevitable bankrupting of the faith.

Do you hear what these critics and even C.S. Lewis are saying?

---

[14] C. S. Lewis, essay "The World's Last Night" (1960), found in *The Essential C.S. Lewis,* Lyle W. Dorsett, ed., (New York: A Touchstone Book, Simon & Schuster, 1996), 385.

Chapter 2

When Did Jesus Say He Would Return?

While talking with his disciples, Jesus told them, *"When you are persecuted in one place, flee to another, I tell you the truth, you will not finish going through the cities of Israel before the Son of man comes"* (Mt. 10:23). And in Matthew 24, *"'Tell us,' they said, 'when will this happen* [destruction of the Temple], *and what will be the sign of your coming* [parousia] *and of the end of the age'"* (vs. 3). That's a simple question – "Tell us when...?" not if, but "when."

Next, Jesus goes into a long answer to their three questions. It includes: the coming of the abomination of desolation standing in the holy place, instructions to flee, great tribulation, sun and moon darkened, stars falling from the sky, heavenly bodies shaken, the coming [*parousia*] of the Son of Man, the sign of the Son of Man appearing in the sky, all the nations of the earth mourning and the Son of Man coming on the clouds of the sky, with power and great glory. Then in verse 34 He answers their time question [*"Tell us...when"*] by declaring, dramatically, *"...I tell you the truth, this generation will certainly not pass away until all these things have happened."*

"What do you do with these passages" (and many others like them), liberals and skeptics ask? Most evangelicals are forced to admit that Jesus didn't return *as* and *when* He promised in that generation, or in that century. They must further concede that his predictions will not be fulfilled within the time parameters he imposed. Instead, standard Christian explanations claim that Jesus' coming has been delayed or postponed, or that the timing was misunderstood, and that He will come again (return) someday "soon" and finish the job. Not only do these attempts evade the plain meaning of clear and emphatic statements, but they actually prove the critics' point.

The informed critics of Christianity have no trouble seeing though the biblical inconsistencies of this poor scholarship. These cover-up attempts just add ammunition to the skeptics' claim—Jesus was incorrect about his time-restricted predictions and therefore cannot be the Messiah. The bottom line is that postponement theories directly contradict the teachings of Jesus, and nonoccurrence leaves Christianity vulnerable to all manner of critical scorn and harmful assaults. It gives the skeptics all the license they need to blaspheme Jesus as not only mistaken and uninspired but as a false prophet or a deceiver as well. It opens wide the door to the dismissal of all Christian claims.

This is exactly the dilemma the liberals, skeptics, Jewish and Muslim critics have forced upon us. Again, it's called "The battle for the Bible." And the focal-point of this attack is the embarrassing time-restricted statements of Jesus about his return, and next, the imminency expectations of the New Testament writers (including other end-time events – resurrection and judgment). Regrettably, this "nonoccurrence" problem cannot be lightly brushed aside without undermining the integrity and divinity of Christ and placing the inerrancy of the Bible in question. It's that simple. It's that profound. And it calls for another reformation of Christianity around a more conservative and biblical view of eschatology.

. . . nonoccurrence leaves
**Christianity vulnerable to all
manner of critical scorn and
harmful assaults.**

Chapter 3

Side-Stepping Devices

Scholars from may different perspectives, including conservative evangelicals, generally agree that Jesus' first followers and every New Testament writer expected his return within their lifetime. They understood Jesus' words, plainly and literally. And no New Testament writer led them to believe any differently, or corrected their widespread understanding.

To their credit, informed liberal and critical scholars know that the phrase "this generation" is used 20 times in the New Testament and is consistent in its meaning—the contemporaries of Jesus.

Conservative prophecy writer and speaker, Thomas Ice, however, does not agree. Ice's futuristic/postponement presuppositions require him to change the normal meaning of "this generation" to mean something different. In his recent book, *The Great Tribulation Past or Future?* (co-authored with Kenneth L. Gentry), Ice writes:

> While it is true that other uses of "this generation" refer to Christ's contemporaries, that is because they are *historical* texts. The use of "this generation" in the Olivet discourse in the fig tree passages are *prophetic* texts. In fact, when one compares the historical use of "this generation" at the beginning of the Olivet

discourse in Matthew 23:36 (which is an undisputed reference to A.D. 70) with the prophetic use in 24:34, a contrast is obvious.[15]

In other words, Ice wants us to believe that everywhere in the New Testament that the word construction "this generation" is used (20 times) it always means the contemporaries of Jesus—*except here*—in Christ's Olivet Discourse.[16] By using this side-stepping, interpretive device, Ice changes the plain and literal meaning of Jesus' "this generation" in these two prophetical texts to mean "that generation"—i.e. whatever future generation sees "all these things" happen will be the generation Jesus meant. Not only is this circular reasoning, it also means, if Ice is correct, that Jesus failed to answer his disciples' "when" question which kicked off this whole discourse.

But before we buy into Ice's explanation, let's take a closer look at the context of Matthew 23:32-36. It immediately precedes and sets the stage for the Olivet Discourse:

> Fill up, then, the measure of the sin of your forefathers! You snakes! You brood of vipers! How will you escape being condemned to hell? Therefore, I am sending you prophets and wise men and teachers. Some of them you will kill and crucify; others you will flog in your synagogues and pursue from town to town. And so upon you will come all the righteous blood that has been shed on earth, from the blood of righteous Abel to the blood of Zechariah son of Berakiah, whom you murdered between the temple and the alter. I tell you the truth, all this will come upon this generation.

Isn't Jesus prophesying of future events here, too? Dr. Kenneth L. Gentry Jr., Ice's co-author, rebuts:

---

[15] Thomas Ice and Kenneth L. Gentry, *The Great Tribulation Past or Future?* (Grand Rapids: Kregel, 1999), 103-104.

[16] Also note that this exception is only for Matthew's and Mark's versions, where the fig tree is mentioned (Mt. 24:32; Mk. 13:28). Luke's version contains no fig tree. Ice concedes that the Luke 21:20-24 portion applies to A.D. 70. – Ibid., 94-95.

Ice tries to distinguish Jesus' use of "this generation" in Matthew 23:36 from the same phrase in 24:34 on the basis that 23:36 is "historical" while 24:34 is "prophetical." But note: (1) *Both* are prophetic. In Matthew 23 Jesus prophesies *future* persecution for his own disciples (23:34) and the catastrophic calamity to befall the Pharisees in A.D. 70 (23:35). Declaring future events in advance is, by definition, "prophetic."[17]

Therefore, Ice's differentiating argument and his interpretation-by-exception hermeneutic both vanish. When we arrive at Matthew 24:34 and find Jesus making the same time-frame reference in a similar declaratory and prophetic statement: "I tell you the truth, this generation will certainly not pass away until all these things have happened." The meaning of "this generation" is identical with, not different from, its uses everywhere else. This time-parameter phrase is consistently used throughout the New Testament. It's an exegetic fact that the critics don't miss.

Furthermore, scholars agree, that Jesus' disciples understood his prophetic words exactly in this way. He spoke to them in the first-person (red letters). They were expected to understand his words (vs 15) and flee (vs 16). This is exactly what they did.[18]

Over the centuries, church leaders have utilized other side-stepping devices to avoid the plain sense of the normal, commonly used and understood words. They have attempted to change the literal meaning of "this generation" to mean:

- "a race of people,"
- "a kind of people"
- "a yet-unborn, distant/future generation"

---

[17] Ice and Gentry, The Great Tribulation Past or Future?, 182.
[18] For more, see this presenter's work – John Noē, *Beyond the End Times: The Rest of...The Greatest Story Ever Told*, (Bradford, PA: International Preterist Association, 1999), 134-142.

- Some claim that Jesus never said these words[19]

Regardless of the side-stepping device employed, informed critics of Christianity have no trouble seeing right though it. These types of literary gymnastics rightfully earn their scorn. It's playing "fast and loose" with the Word of God. It does not answer the charges. And, in this presenter's opinion, it is a classic, modern example of how the traditions of men can "nullify the word of God by your tradition . . . and you do many things like that," or make it of "none effect" (Mk. 7:13; Mt. 15:6 – NIV-KJV).

Let's face it, these critics have a legitimate complaint if Jesus did not do something that He said He would. The tactics of manipulating or tampering with the normal meaning of common words, and interrupting time parameters to force fit a futuristic/postponement position, are blatant admissions of weakness. They are also errors and expose a vulnerability ripe for exploitation by critics and opponents.

Let's face it, these critics have a legitimate complaint if Jesus did not do something that He said He would.

---

[19] Ibid., 113-127.

Chapter 4

Taking It Seriously

With origins in the 19th-century Enlightenment, the liberal/skeptical intrusion upon the Scriptures and Christianity has operated with a boldness of criticism that has infiltrated the thinking of far too many professors, seminary students, pastors, and pew sitters. Time and again, the supposed failure of the eschatological events to occur in Jesus' 1st-century generation is brought up as the reason they reject the inspiration and authority of Christ and the New Testament.

Fact is, Jesus made clear, concrete, future predictions about his coming in glory that seemingly did not come to pass. Or so we've been told. Liberal criticism, especially, concentrates on that point. They are more than aware of the dilemma which nonoccurrence presents for the Christian Church and the impossibility of escaping it without being disloyal to Christ. Their weighty criticism, truly, should be a "cause for pause" for anyone who believes in the inspiration and authority of Scripture. The integrity of Christ and all the New Testament writers is at stake.

No one has articulated this matter better and more seriously than the respected Reformed theologian, R.C. Sproul:

> ". . . the skepticism expressed by [Bertrand] Russell on these matters is by no means limited to him, but is the axe that is ground by a host of higher-critical scholars of the Bible. . . .the chief ground for the radical criticism of modern biblical

scholarship, which has resulted in a wholesale attack on the trustworthiness of Scripture and a far-reaching skepticism . . . is the thesis that the Gospels' records of Jesus' predictions contain glaring errors and gross inaccuracies. . . . The problem, however, is that Russell's is not a lone voice in recent history. His criticisms are echoed by a multitude of highly learned specialists in the field of biblical studies. . . . In seminary I was exposed daily to critical theories espoused by my professors regarding the Scriptures. What stands out in my memory of those days is the heavy emphasis on biblical texts regarding the return of Christ, which were constantly cited as examples of errors in the New Testament and proof that the text had been edited to accommodate the crisis in the early church caused by the so-called parousia-delay of Jesus.[20]

Yet, conservative evangelicals have tried to whitewash over the immensity of this problem, hoping to obscure it from fellow evangelicals and remove in from serious consideration. But this crisis won't go away. Fact is, we have not taken this cancerous infiltration seriously enough. Nor have we crafted a credible or effective response. Hence, the liberals, skeptics, and critics are winning by our default.

Once again, R.C. Sproul sums up this dilemma rather well:

It is my fear that evangelicals today tend to underplay the significance of the problems inherent in Russell's assumptions.[21]

One of the most critical issues that the Church faces today and has been facing for some time, and that is, a serious crisis . . . in the area of eschatology. . . . a wholesale attack on the trustworthiness of the Bible and of the truth of the Scripture concerning the Person and work of Jesus Himself. . . . I have never been satisfied that the evangelical community has dealt with the problems of the time-frame references that are set forth

---

[20] R.C. Sproul, *The Last Days According to Jesus* (Grand Rapids: Baker Books, 1998), 14-15.
[21] R.C. Sproul, The Last Days According to Jesus, 17.

in the New Testament about the near-term expectations . . .
things that were to happen within the first century.[22]

. . . skeptical criticism of the Bible has become almost universal
in the world. And people have attacked the credibility of Jesus.
Maybe some Church fathers made a mistake. Maybe our
favorite theologians have made mistakes. I can abide with that.
I can't abide with Jesus being a false prophet, because if I am to
understand that Jesus is a false prophet, my faith is in vain.[23]

The evangelical world cannot afford to turn a deaf ear to the
railing voices of skepticism that gut Scripture of its divine
authority, that assault the credibility of the apostolic witness and
even of Christ himself. We must take seriously the skeptic's
critique of the time-frame references of New Testament
prophecy, and we must answer them convincingly.[24]

The integrity of Christ and all the New Testament writers is at stake.

---

[22] R.C. Sproul, "Last Days Madness" presentation, Ligonier Ministries' National Conference 1999.
Cassette.

[23] R.C. Sproul, "The Problem of Imminency" presentation, Covenant Eschatology Symposium, Mt.
Dora, FL. 1993. Cassette.

[24] R.C. Sproul, *The Last Days According to Jesus*, 203.

Chapter 5

The Only Solution to the Problem of "Nonoccurrence"

How can conservative evangelicals "answer them convincingly"? Certainly, it's not with the postponement theories of the past, or by changing the meaning of commonly understood and normally used words, or by any of the other side-stepping techniques futurists are forced to employ. Nor can we continue to ignore these attacks hoping they will go away. They won't.

Nor can we answer "convincingly" by publishing more "four-views" books:

> There are a number of books...on four views [such as *Revelation Four Views*]. They are important steps on moving toward consensus and toward a solution on a problem. But they are by definition not the solution. . . . Somehow we need to work at establishing a distinctive evangelical scholarly voice. There's a Jewish voice. And there's a Roman Catholic voice. And there's a liberal academic voice. But there is no distinctly evangelical academic voice. We lose by default...Consider the possibility that God wants the Church to discover answers and reach consensus on more and more problems . . . to speak with a unified voice on certain issues and before the whole world.[25]

---

[25] Wayne Grudem , "Do We Act like We Really Believe That 'The Bible Alone, and the Bible in its Entirety, Is the Word of God Written'?" Presidential Address," Evangelical Theological Society's 51st Annual Meeting in Danvers, MA, 1999. The use of Dr. Grudem's quote should not be construed as an endorsement of the view this book presents.

Are we so blind to the implications of nonoccurrence? Again, the very credibility of Jesus and authority of Scripture are at stake. We must come to grips with the inspired time-frame parameters and Jesus' inclusion of his *parousia* return within the context of his "all these things."

Only one generation in human history is, was, or will be the generation to experience the return of Jesus. Is it possible that there is a relatively simple yet greatly overlooked solution to this discrediting problem of nonocuurence? Perhaps the most obvious has been staring us in the face all these centuries.

The *only solution* to the problem of "nonoccurrence" is *occurrence*! It's the only biblically *consistent solution* that can stop the liberal/skeptic attack dead in its tracks. It's also the simplest solution. It has been right in front of us all along. And that is—*Jesus was correct*. He said what He meant and meant what He said. This means that 1st-century imminency expectations proved true. In other words:

- Everything Jesus said would happen happened, exactly *as* and *when* He said it would.
- Everything every New Testament writer expected to happen happened, exactly *as* and *when* they expected.

Isn't this a most-compelling argument? Isn't it more Christ-honoring, Scripture-authenticating, and faith-validating than postponement or we-just-can't know theories? Is it really so unbearable to believe that everything happened exactly *as* and *when* Jesus predicted it would and every New Testament writer expected? After all, they were guided into all truth and shown the things that were to come (Jn. 16:13). Perhaps, we are the ones who must learn to honor the clearly used, consistently employed, and biblically defined time parameters that Scripture imposes upon itself, and, consequently, adjust our understanding of the nature of prophecy's precise past fulfillment.

This is the Preterist position. It documents how all eschatological events came to pass within the lifetime of Jesus' contemporaries—i.e., within his "this generation" and in that same, uninterrupted "last days" time frame (Heb. 1:1-2). This includes our Lord's time-restricted return. Nothing was delayed, nothing proved false, everything certainly came to pass (Hab. 2:3; Heb. 10:37), right on time, and in conjunction with the fall of Jerusalem in A.D. 70.

For this reason and more, the Preterist position is the most Christ-honoring, Scripture-authenticating, and faith-validating of all six major eschatological views in the historic Church. I encourage you to honestly and sincerely consider the great advantage the Preterist view has in combating the liberal/skeptic attack on the Bible. Surely, it is "the only solution." Without it, evangelicals are left with no credible response.

Today, the time is more than ripe for conservative evangelicals to discover the beauty of our literal, "once-for-all-delivered" and completely fulfilled faith (Jude 3). Only with the strength of the Preterist approach, can we rise to the ideological challenge and counterattack with something of substance. It's the only way we can answer "convincingly," as R.C. Sproul has admonished. The Preterist view takes Jesus at his word and every New Testament writer at his word, as well. What they expected, apparently, was what they were shown (Jn. 16:13). If they were wrong about something as important as this, how can we trust them to convey other aspects of the faith along to us correctly—such as the requirements for salvation, etc.? But they were not wrong.

This is the strength the Preterist view brings to the battle. I recommend it to your serious attention, and so do others:

"I am encouraging my students and colleagues
to carefully consider the Preterist view."

– L. Rush Bush, *past-President ETS*, from
comments made in the International Presterist
Association's exhibit booth at the 51st Annual
Meeting of the Evangelical Theological Society
in Danvers, MA, 1999. (Used by permission)

**Are we so blind to the implications
of nonoccurrence? Again, the
very credibility of Jesus and
authority of Scripture are at
stake.**

Chapter 6

Differing Opinions about Preterism

When a Christian first hears a statement that all Bible prophecy has been fulfilled and Jesus has returned (past tense), he or she, most likely, will react in a knee-jerk fashion, exclaiming:

"You believe what?"

"Are you crazy?"

After all, it is so different. For so long, we've become accustomed to just the opposite view, and we don't like our boat rocked. We think this futuristic/postponement view serves our needs quite well, when it really doesn't.

Admittedly, the Preterist position is not well known today. But this is changing, thanks for one to R.C. Sproul's recent book about Preterism titled, *The Last Days According to Jesus*. Although he is not yet in full agreement, Dr. Sproul has nonetheless encouraged serious consideration of Preterism as perhaps the best solution to the nonfulfillment dilemma posed by liberals and skeptics. In the conclusion of his book, Dr. Sproul writes:

> The purpose of *The Last Days According to Jesus* has been to examine and evaluate the various claims of preterism, both full and partial. The great service preterism performs is to focus attention on two major issues. The first is the time-frame references of the New Testament regarding eschatological prophecy. The preterist is a

sentinel standing guard against frivolous and superficial attempts to downplay or explain away the force of these references.

The second major issue is the destruction of Jerusalem. This event certainly spelled the end of a crucial redemptive-historical epoch. It must be viewed as the end of some age. It also represents a significant visitation of the Lord in judgment and a vitally important "day of the Lord." Whether this was the *only* day of the Lord about which Scripture speaks remains a major point of controversy among preterists.[26]

But differing opinions about Preterism exist in the conservative evangelical community. Thomas Ice, for one, would not agree with Dr. Sproul's favorable comments above. Ice does not believe that Preterism in any form is a valid position to hold. In a *Midnight Call* magazine article, Oct. 99, he called preterism "a strange view."[27] In the June 1999 issue, he termed it "a strange new fad within the field of Bible Prophecy."[28] In his recent book, *The Great Tribulation Past or Future?*, he called "full" or "consistent" Preterism—which this writer represents— "heretical" and "heterodox."[29]

In a public debate between Dr. Ice and myself last November on the topic of "Preterist *vs.* Futurist," he closed the debate, thusly: "I want to close this debate by appealing to John [me] to repent of his error of misinterpretation of Scripture and come back into the fold of orthodoxy."[30] Some futurists even point to the rise of Preterism as another strong proof of the truth of

---

[26] R.C. Sproul, *The Last Days According to Jesus*, 202-203.
[27] Thomas Ice, "Has Bible Prophecy Already Been Fulfilled? Part V," *Midnight Call Magazine*, October 1999, 22.
[28] Thomas Ice, "Has Bible Prophecy Already Been Fulfilled?," *Midnight Call Magazine*, June 1999, 23.
[29] Ice and Gentry, *The Great Tribulation Past or Future?*, 163.
[30] John Noē vs. Tommy Ice, "Preterist *vs.* Futurist," sponsored by Families Against Cults of Indiana, November 1999. Cassette.

futurism—i.e., they try to paint Preterism as part of the great end-time apostasy the Bible predicts (2Th. 2:3; 2Pe. 3:3-4). One of the many problems with this ad hominem, self-serving tactic is, it's 19 centuries off on its timing. Unfortunately, words like "heretic" or "heterodoxy" or "apostasy" flow far too easily off the tongues of many Christians in their effort to maintain their system of belief in the face of a challenging view. Naturally, we need to be discerning. But then being discerning is why rapidly growing numbers of conservative futurists are gravitating to the preterist position. Almost every preterist I know, including myself, started out as a futurist.

Dr. Ice is right about two things in his book, however. (1) He writes that Preterism is enjoying "significant growth."[31] (2) "Until recently, futurism has enjoyed an unobstructed field. Preterism, the polar opposite of futurism, has arisen at least to provide a challenge to the futurist dominance within evangelicalism...The debate is shaping up as a showdown between preterism and futurism."[32]

I agree. But how many more seminaries, churches, and believers have to fall victim to the liberal/skeptic attack on the Bible before we are willing to respond with something of substance? It's far past time for we evangelicals to wake up, stop abdicating this ground to our opponents, and honestly deal with this destructive onslaught, head on. A new reformation awaits us!

---

[31] Ice and Gentry, *The Great Tribulation Past or Future?*, 7.
[32] Ibid., 6.

But how many more seminaries, churches, and believers have to fall victim to the liberal/skeptic attack on the Bible before we are willing to respond with something of substance?

Chapter 7

The Case for Occurrence—a Brief Overview

The New Testament contains dozens of time reference and imminency texts. Many of these are cited by the liberals to call into question the inspiration and authority of the Bible. It is here that the inconsistencies of the futuristic/ postponement positions are most embarrassingly exposed. In this section, we will highlight ten key texts. But first, put yourself in the shoes of the original audience and think about these three questions:

1. Why were the New Testament writers talking like this in that 1st Century?

2. If you were living back then, how would you have understood these words?

3. How do you think Jesus' contemporaries understood these words?

Come now, let us reason together" (Isa. 1:18). What was so urgent, so significant, and so imminent? Truth is what we're after.

Hebrews 1:2 – *"but in these last days he [God] has spoken to us by his Son,..."*

Clearly and by divine inspiration, the writer of Hebrews—who was writing some twenty or thirty years after Jesus' crucifixion—affixes the biblical time period known as the "last days" to the time of Jesus' earthly ministry and to the time in which he was writing. He saw himself living in the "last days," back then and there. He said "in *these* last days," not "in *those* last days." Big difference. But they were the "last days" of what? They were the "last days," the "last time" (1Pe. 1:5), "these last times" (1Pe. 1:20), and "last hour" (1Jn. 2:18) of the biggest thing that was ending at the time or ever will end on planet Earth and in redemptive and world history.

What was it? I'll give you a clue. It wasn't the end of the world—because the world is without end (Eph. 3:21 KJV; Eccl. 1:4; Ps. 78:69; 104:5; 93:1; 96:10; 119:90; also true for the moon, sun, and highest heavens – see Ps. 89:36-37; Ps. 148:4,6). Likewise, "For God did not send his Son into the world to condemn the world..."(Jn. 3:17). And neither should we by saying that it is going to end someday. Scripture clearly teaches that God's creation is eternally established, i.e., without end. Yet, "these last days" weren't the "last days" of the Christian age. It was the beginning days of the Church.

Be assured that the proper time placement of the biblical time period known as the "last days" is key. Furthermore, our realization of its significance will unravel much of the confusion in Christendom over the end times and provide us with a correct foundation for understanding other end-time events, such as resurrection and judgment.

Mark 1:15 – *"The time is fulfilled..." (KJV)*

What "time" was Jesus talking about that He claimed was "fulfilled?" It was the final time of the greatest time prophecy ever given to humankind—Daniel's seventy weeks of years (Da. 9:24-27). The 70th week, a 7-year period of covenantal confirmation was upon them, then and there—no gaps, no interruptions.

This divinely determined time frame began with the decree of Artaxerxes in 457 B.C. Then, "at just the right time" (Ro. 5:6), 483 years later in A.D. 27, the Messiah was publicly recognized as "the Anointed One" (Da. 9:25) with Jesus' baptism in the Jordan River. This anointing event marks the beginning of Daniel's 70th and final week. That is why Jesus made the statement, "the time is fulfilled" (Mk. 1:15 KJV). The next 7 years (one week) were to be a time of covenantal confirmation. This is the described nature for the 70th week, not a time of world tribulation. Big difference! In the middle of this week, in A.D. 30, the Messiah was "cut off," crucified (Da. 9:26, 27). By A.D. 34, Daniel's 70-weeks time prophecy was completely fulfilled. The time God had determined or decreed upon Daniel's people, the Jews, was over. The gospel was now freed to go to the Gentiles. The event that marks the end of this 70th week occurred when "Philip went down to a city in Samaria, and proclaimed Christ there" (Ac. 8:5)—something Christ had previously forbidden (Mt. 10:5-6; 15:24). Wasn't Philip, and later Peter and John (Ac. 8:14f), being disobedient by going there? The answer is no. The time restriction for confirming the New Covenant exclusively upon the Jews was now chronologically over.

Hence, Daniel's entire 70 weeks time prophecy transpired over an uninterrupted 490-year period. Yet most Christians have been taught otherwise:

Christians, for lack of a better answer, claim that the 70th week will take place when Jesus returns in his second coming as a king. The problem was caused because Daniel mentioned a total of 70 weeks, and then he specified 7 plus 62, leaving one remaining. The Christians say that the first 69 weeks were consecutive, then there is at least a *1900 year gap*, and sooner or later the 70th week will occur. This is obviously a very forced explanation, born of desperation.[33]

Sadly to say, Levine is right. Not only is Daniel 9 one of, if not arguably, the most important chapter in the Bible, but, without a doubt, it is the most misunderstood and misapplied. Daniel's 70 weeks' prophecy says nothing about an interruption or gap between any of its weeks or a 7-year period of tribulation or a coming antichrist. This time frame was fulfilled, exactly, literally, chronologically, and sequentially. Its perfect fulfillment is now part of the history and heritage of our "once-for-all-delivered faith" (Jude 3). It has no bearing on our future, except that it is far past time we reform our traditional but erroneous interruptions.[34]

1Corinthians 7:29 – *"Time is short"*

We hear this statement a lot nowadays from the "Left Behind" crowd. But these words were penned in the 1st Century. Whose time was short back then?

---

[33] Samuel Levine, You Take Jesus, I'll Take God: How To Refute Christian Missionaries (Los Angeles: Hamoroh Press, 1980), 31.

[34] For an amplified explanation of the exact, literal, chronological, and sequential fulfillment of Daniel's 70 weeks—no gaps, no gimmicks—see presenter's book, *Beyond the End Times*, Chapter 6, 71-89.

1Corinthians 7:31 – *"The world in its present form is passing away"*

What world was passing away back then? The answer to that question is at the *heart* of what Bible eschatology is all about.

Galatians 4:4 – *"The fullness of time was come"*

What "fullness" of what "time" was Paul talking about? If back then was the "fullness," does time ever get any more full? One thing this means is, there was no element of delay, postponement, or interruption.

Luke 21:20, 22 – *"When you see Jerusalem surrounded by armies...this is the time of punishment in fulfillment of all that has been written."*

Four times after Jesus said these words, and within the generation of his contemporaries, Jerusalem was surrounded by armies.

"All that has been written" means the whole Old Testament (see Lk. 24:44). Especially note that Jesus did not say "some of what has been written." He said "all." That means all of Daniel and his 70 weeks and "time of the end" time prophecies, and all of Isaiah and his coming of the "new heavens and a new earth" (Isa. 65:17-18; 66:22), and more. Whether we recognize it, understand it, or not, this is the plain, literal meaning of these words of Jesus.

1Corinthians 10:11 – *"The fulfillment of the ages has come"*
Yes, something very significant was upon them, then and there.

1John 2:18 – *"Little children, this is the last hour...it is the last hour."*

Twice John says it. He doesn't say it "might be" or "someday will be" but "it is." Who can deny it? The "last hour" was upon them. But the "last hour" of what?

Hebrews 10:37 – *"In just a very little while, 'He who is coming will come and will not delay...'"*

But the Church has been preaching delay for 19 centuries and counting! Who's right? Let's stick with the inspired writer of Hebrews.

Our postponing brethren, however, tell us that the Lord's return and other end-time events (judgment and resurrection) are always viewed as being imminent. If they are right, then these time statements we've been highlighting in this section are meaningless. But how far can you stretch imminency before imminency looses its value?

1Pet 4:7 – *"The end of all things is at hand." (KJV)*

This is the clincher, in this presenter's opinion. Notice that this wording is not "the end of *some* things" or "the *middle* of all things," but "the end of all things." "At hand" is the Greek word *engys*. It's an idom and means "graspable, seizible, there for the taking." For example, Jesus used it when He said:

- "behold, the hour is at hand" for his betrayal (Mt. 26:45)
- the one who betrays me is "at hand" (Mt. 26:46)

- "the kingdom of God is at hand" (Mk. 1:15), and sent his 12 disciples out to proclaim the same thing (Mt. 10:7)
- John said the Jews' passover was "at hand" (Jn. 11:55)

It's the ultimate imminency idiom.

Thomas Ice, my previously referred to opponent in a recent "Preterist *vs.* Futurist" debate, agrees that the idiom *engys,* "at hand," *usually* means something that will take place within a short span of time. But then he says that it doesn't have to mean this everywhere. The only evidence he cites is an illustration from sports:

> It is true that *engys* can be and often is used to refer to something that takes place within a short span of time from when it is stated. Yet there are other instances when *engys* refers to something as "at hand," or "within reach"; but this does not mean that it must take place soon. An illustration from sports may help. A team may make it to the championship game. It may be said of that team that the championship is "at hand" or "within grasp." This does not mean that it is certain to come within a short period of time, just because it is at hand. Just ask the Buffalo Bills. The NFL championship has been "near" or "at hand" for a number of year for the Bills, but thus far it has yet to arrive.[35]

In our debate, I read this above paragraph from his book and asked Dr. Ice, What kind of Bible scholarship is this? The reason Ice does not cite any scriptural examples to support his alternative meaning is, there are none. Nowhere in its many uses in the New Testament is the Greek idiomatic word *engys,* translated as "at hand" or "near," ever used in the alternative way Ice contends. It is consistent in its meaning, just as is "this generation."

---

[35] Ice and Gentry, *The Great Tribulation Past or Future?,* 115.

So what "end" was Peter talking about that was "at hand" back then and there? These are *not complicated words*. Again, ask yourself, if you were living back then, how would you have understood them? And just how much of this was relevant to its original audience? According Ice and his premillennial view, "none of it" was. According to the amillennialist and historicist, "some of it" was. According to the postmillennialist, "most of it" was. But according to the preterist view, "all of it" was relevant and fulfilled, right on time.

Seriously, if the expectations of every New Testament writers about these very significant issues proved wrong and fulfillment hasn't happen for 19-centuries- and-counting, how can we trust them to convey other aspects of the faith to us accurately? And remember, they were specifically given the Holy Spirit to "guide you into all truth" and to "tell you what is to come" (Jn. 16:13). Rather, why don't we just take these inspired writers at their word, simply, plainly, and literally? And, while at it, let's take Jesus at his word, too? In the words of the first two lines of the old church song, *Tis So Sweet*:

Tis So Sweet to trust in Jesus
Just to take Him at His word

Problems is, most interpreters have been unwilling to do that. Nor are they willing to take these above time statements literally. So, what's the scoop? Why were Jesus and these New Testament writers talking like this? What was so monumental and so imminent, right then and there in their lifetime, to justify such strong, emphatic claims?

Again, ask yourself, if you were
living back then, how would you
have understood them?

Chapter 8

Daniel's "Time of the End"

Seven centuries before Christ, God inspired the Old Testament prophet Habakkuk to write:

> For the revelation awaits an appointed time; it speaks of the end and will not prove false. Though it linger, wait for it; it will certainly come and will not delay. <u>Habakkuk 2:3</u>

There's that word again, "time." Get the idea? Time is important to God. It is something He wants us to understand. So let's understand this. The "appointed time of the end" would *not prove false*. It would *certainly come* and would *not delay*! Do you hear that? Yet for 19-centuries-and-counting many in the Church have been teaching delay or postponement, as if God didn't know about Isaiah 53 and the future rejection of the Messiah by his own people.

However, at the time Habakkuk wrote, neither he nor any one had any idea when this "appointed time...of the end" (not "end of time"—big difference) would happen, or what events would accompany it.

One century later, using another Old Testament prophet, God filled in more details. This included the revealing of the *defining characteristic* and the *historical setting* for the one-and-only "end" the Bible consistently proclaims:

But you, Daniel, close up and seal the words of the scroll until the time of the end…It will be for a time, times and half a time. When the power of the holy people has been finally broken, all these things will be completed." Daniel 12:4,7

Who were the holy people when Daniel wrote? The Jews! Who were they when Jesus was crucified? Again, the Jews! Who were they when the New Testament books were written? Once again, the Jews! What was their power? It was the biggest power any group of people ever had or will ever have here on planet Earth. It was the Jews' exclusive relationship with God as manifested by their temple complex.

The final breaking of this power was to be the *historical setting* and the *defining characteristic* for Daniel's "time of the end." This is exactly what happened in the destruction of Jerusalem and the Temple in A.D 70. The Jew's power started to be broken at the cross, or, perhaps, with Christ's birth. But it couldn't be "finally broken" until the old was completed removed (Mt. 5:17-18; Heb. 9:8-10) and left forever "desolate" (Mt. 23:38). That "end" came. It was covenantal, and not cosmic. And all associated end-time events took place within the literal "this generation" of Jesus' contemporaries—exactly *as* and *when* He said it would—when "the power of the holy people" was "finally broken."

Now you know the reason the pre-A.D.-70, inspired New Testament writers were making such startling, consummatory statements. The fulfillment of all end-time prophecy—from the Old Testament to the New Testament—fits together like a glove, perfectly and harmoniously, when kept in its divinely determined 1st-century timeframe. We preterists call this consistency. Doesn't this exactness glorify God more than interruptions,

postponement gaps, and other side-stepping devices and
gimmicks?[36]

The challenge we next must address in this book is
explaining how the Lord literally and bodily came again, returned,
during this fulfilled "time of the end." After all, no one physically
saw Him do it.

**Get the idea? Time is important
to God. It is something He wants
us to understand.**

---

[36] For an amplified explanation of the exact, literal, chronological, and sequential fulfillment of
Daniel's "time of the end" and its "1,290" and "1,335 days" timeframe (Da. 12:11-12)—no gaps, no
gimmicks —see presenter's book, *Beyond the End Times*, Chapters 7 & 8, 91-109.

Chapter 9

Christ's Coming on the Clouds—a Long Biblical Precedent[37]

Jesus specified exactly *how* He would come again (i.e., the nature of his *parousia* coming). Twice He said He would come "on the clouds" (Mt. 24:30; 26:64). But what did He mean? If you were a 1st-century Jew raised in the synagogue, you would have known exactly what it meant. This type of coming had a long biblical precedent. To appreciate the rich Jewish terminology for cloud-coming, we must enter the mind of a 1st-century Jew. If we look at these things only through 21st-century eyes, we'll become prisoners of what has become the traditional mindset of misunderstanding and confusion.

Christ's "coming on the clouds" is a common metaphor borrowed from Old Testament portrayals of God descending from heaven and coming in power and glory to execute judgment on a people or nation. In all the historic comings of God in judgment, He acted through human armies, or through nature, to bring destruction ("the Lord is a man of war" [Ex. 15:3 KJV]). Each was a direct act of God and each was termed "the day of the Lord." They were always described with figurative language, and empowered by supernatural support, and they brought historical

---

[37] The material in this and the next chapter, excluding the outside source quotes, is borrowed from Ibid.,182-185, 187-191.

calamity to Egypt, Edom, Assyria, Babylon, and even on Israel itself.

The Jews of Jesus' day had studied these "day of the Lord" occurrences and were familiar with "cloud-coming" phraseology, as well as the application of one with the other.[38] The Hebrew scriptures are rich in similes and figurative language that poetically portray a heavenly perspective of God coming among men in judgment:

- See, the Lord rides on a swift *cloud* and is coming to Egypt (Isa. 19:1). (For the earthly fulfillment, see Isaiah 20:1-6)
- Look! He advances like the *clouds,* his chariots come like a whirlwind (Jer. 4:13).
- For the day is near, the day of the Lord is near—a day of *clouds*, a time of doom for the nations (Eze. 30:3).
- Sing to God, sing praise to his name, extol him who rides on the *clouds*... (Ps. 68:4).
- ... He makes the *clouds* his chariots and rides on the wings of the wind. He makes winds his messengers, flames of fire his servants (Ps. 104:3-4).

---

[38] Also, in the Old Testament, God dwelt in, or was present in, a physical and visible Shekhinah glory cloud. This is an entirely different matter and will not be addressed here. Our interest is how cloud phraseology is used in a symbolic manner in both prophetic and apocalyptic eschatology, namely that of swiftness and power of literal judgment.

Some interpreters contend that Acts 1:11's account of Jesus ascending into a cloud and two angels declaring that He would come back in "like manner" or "in the same way you have seen Him go into heaven" requires that He return visibly on a physical cloud(s). What's missed here is an equal argument that can be made from this same passage to support the *invisibility* of Christ at his return, since "a cloud hid him from their sight" (v. 9) before He entered heaven. This cloud was not an application in the same pattern of "cloud-coming" judgment. "Like manner" or "same way" refers to how He comes (i.e., the means of), which is in and out of the spirit realm, manifesting Himself in numerous forms and places for a wide variety of purposes. That has always been the way Jesus' many comings happened throughout both the Old and New Testament. The manner of Jesus' many comings is beyond the scope of this book. Those interested will find more on this topic in my paper, *The Many Comings of Jesus*, presented at the 49th Annual Meeting of the Evangelical Theological Society in November of 1997 in Santa Clara, California.

- Also see Eze. 30:18; Ps. 18:9-12; 2Sa. 22:10-12; Na. 1:3; Joel 2:1-2; Zep. 1:14-15).

With familiar cloud-coming imagery Daniel prophesied the coming of the Son of Man (Da. 7:13). Jesus, by deriving his "coming on the clouds" phrase directly from Daniel, was revealing Himself as God and the promised Messiah (Mt. 24:30; 26:64). The high priest Caiaphas immediately understood this claim of Jesus to be Deity and responded, "He has spoken blasphemy!" (Mt. 26:65). Jesus was also applying his coming in judgment and power of war in the *same* technical way as the Father had come down from Heaven many times before:

> Look! The Lord is coming from his dwelling place;
> he comes down and treads the high places of the earth
> (Mic. 1:3).

> See, the Lord is coming out of his dwelling to punish
> the people of the earth for their sins (Isa. 26:21).

> But your many enemies will become like fine dust,
> the ruthless hordes like blown chaff.
> Suddenly, in an instant the Lord Almighty will come
> with thunder and earthquake and great noise, with
> windstorm and tempest and flames of a devouring fire
> (Isa. 29:5-6).

Because of this background, Jesus' disciples would have understood what He was talking about in his Olivet Discourse (Mt. 24:30). The high priest understood it. That's why he was so offended by and accused Jesus of blasphemy (Mt. 26:64-65). Let's note that Jesus made no disclaimers to change the meaning or nature of this type of coming, and neither should we.

Another important factor is that in all these real biblical comings of God in the Old Testament, God was *never physically visible*; He was unseen by human eyes! Thus, cloud-coming is the language of divine imagery. It denotes divine action. In every instance, humans were fully aware of God's Presence and personal intervention in those events of history. Obviously, this Jewish perspective is quite different from the way we moderns have been conditioned to think of Christ's coming on the clouds. We imagine his coming to be spectacularly visible on the tops of literal fluffy cumulus clouds transporting Him down to earth.[39] Yet every biblical instance of a cloud-coming was a real coming of God. Jesus employed the same figure of speech for his end-time prophecies. Thus for Jesus and a 1st-century Jew, coming "on the clouds" was not a claim to come visibly to the human eye.

With this understanding, we can see the Lord Jesus making his appearance, or coming again, in the events of the Roman-Jewish War and the final destruction of Jerusalem in A.D. 70. Just as the cloud-coming Jehovah God came in Old Testament times, Jesus came "in the clouds." He came utilizing the armies of Rome to deliver his people. And in keeping with the Old Testament pattern, He was not physically seen. Kenneth L. Gentry agrees:

> This cloud-coming of Christ in judgment is reminiscent of Old Testament cloud-comings of God in judgment upon ancient historical people and nations.
>
> The final collapse of Jerusalem and the Temple. . . .Through these events the Jews were to "see" the Son of Man in His judgment-coming in terrifying cloud-glory: clouds are symbols of divine majesty often entailing stormy destruction. . . . The members of the Sanhedrim and others would experience such in their life times (Matt. 26:64; Mark 9:1; cf. Rev. 1:7 with Rev. 1:1, 3).[40]

---

[39] To be consistent, shouldn't we also think of Him coming on a white horse (Rev. 19:11), as riding on a literal four-legged steed?

[40] Kenneth L. Gentry, *He Shall Have Dominion* (Tyler, TX: Institute for Christian Economics, 1992) 388-389, 348.

Another important fact to reflect in this judgment event is the change of covenant. Therefore, "the day of the Lord" (Jehovah) of the Old Testament became "the day of Christ" (*Christos* 2Th. 2:2; *kurios* 2Pe. 3:10) in the New Testament.

Look, he is coming with the clouds (Rev. 1:7).

Obviously, this Jewish perspective is quite different from the way we moderns have been conditioned to think of Christ's coming on the clouds.

Chapter 10

In the Same Way, for the Same Purpose

Jesus came in judgment against an apostate Judaism. James told his readers that "the judge is standing at the door!" (Jas. 5:9). Peter wrote plainly, "For it is time for judgment to begin with the family of God" (1Pe. 4:17). Modern interpretations leave Judge Jesus standing at the door!

But Jesus' coming in A.D. 70 involved both visible and invisible aspects. Using the language of the Prophets, and comparing the biblical precedents of a coming "day of the Lord," we can document how Jesus' coming was accomplished. He came in exactly the same *way* ("on the clouds"), for exactly the same *purpose* (judgment), to accomplish exactly the same *thing* (destruction of a nation).

First, history records—quite literally—that Jerusalem and the Temple were destroyed by invading Roman armies in A.D. 70. "Not one stone [was] left upon another," just as Jesus had said (Mt. 24:2). Jesus had inseparably connected his coming with this dramatically visible, historical event (Mt. 24:1-34). This linkage of time, event, and place in his Olivet Discourse prophecy cannot be overstated. Even the 1st-century scoffers knew that the Temple's destruction was the corresponding physical event that signaled his coming (2Pe. 3:3-4).

Second, the prophet Ezekiel said that in the latter days God would come up against Israel "as a cloud to cover the land" (Eze. 38:9, 16; see also Zec. 12-14). New Testament writers confirmed they were then living in those "last days" (Heb. 1:2; Ac. 2:17; 1Ti. 4:1; 2Ti. 3:1; Jas. 5:3; 2Pe. 3:3; 1Pe. 1:5, 20; Jude 18; 1Jn. 2:18). At this time, Isaiah had prophesied, the Messiah would come robed "with the garments of vengeance for clothing" (Isa. 59:17f; see also Ro. 12:19), and He would proclaim not only salvation, but "the day of vengeance of our God" (Isa. 61:2). Jesus' statement in Luke's account of the Olivet Discourse contains this very wording: "When you [Jesus' audience] see Jerusalem surrounded by armies, you will know that its desolation is near...flee... For this is the time of punishment [*these be the days of vengeance*] in fulfillment of all that has been written" (Lk. 21:20-22 [in *KJV*]). The immediate historical setting and explicit framework for these happenings proved to be the Jewish-Roman War of A.D. 66 – 70. After A.D. 70, the "last days" were over.

Third, Isaiah foretold that during this time Israel would fill up the measure of her sin and she would be destroyed (Isa. 65:6-15) by the Lord, who would come with fire and judgment (Isa. 66:15f). Jesus said that this time of filling up would "come upon this generation" (Mt. 23:32-36). That 1st-century apostate Jewish nation, with its city and Temple, had become the great enemy of God's emerging new people, the Church.

Jesus, Ezekiel, Isaiah, and Daniel precisely pinpointed when everything promised would come to pass. If they were wrong, they weren't inspired. There is no valid way to escape it. As the time approached, James said, "The coming of the Lord is at hand" (Jas. 5:8 NAS). Paul reminded his first readers that "the time is short" (1Cor. 7:29). Peter proclaimed, "The end of all things is at hand" (1Pe. 4:7 KJV), and warned, "For the time has come for judgment to begin at the house of God" (1Pe. 4:17). Urgency permeates Peter's sense of expectation. He is emphatic, "The time has come!" John wrote, "It is the last hour!" (1Jn. 2:18b). How many "last hours" can there be? How long is short? How could these statements be more clear? How many declarations are required before we can believe this inspired imminency?

Fourth, the "sign" of his invisible coming would be:

> Do you see all these things?' he asked. 'I tell you the truth not one stone here will be left on another; every one will be thrown down (Mt. 24:2)

The destruction of Jerusalem and its Temple was the "sign" (Mt. 24:3). The "sign of the Son of Man ... in the sky [in heaven]" (Mt. 24:30) could have been the plumes of smoke arising from the burning fires above the mountain plateau on which Jerusalem sat (Mk. 10:33).[41] The destruction of the Judaic world followed the same pattern and nature of many Old Testament comings of God, or "days of the Lord." In every instance of God's intervention, his Presence was there, but He was never actually seen.

Let's recall that God had set Jerusalem on a high place (Ps. 48:1-2; Isa. 2:2-3) at the crossroads of the world (three continents) and "in the center of the nations, with countries all around her" (Eze. 5:5-17). He had a definite purpose (see Eze. 5:8-17). After the fall of A.D. 70, transcontinental traders and travelers from near and far could readily see that something significant had happened. News of the devastation of God's chosen people, their Temple, and the entire nation thus spread rapidly throughout the Roman world.

Let's likewise note that Jesus did not appear "in person." His resurrected body did not appear in the sky to signal this special coming, nor will it. Yet his bodily Presence was there, in keeping with the long-standing day-of-the-Lord motif. That's why a sign was needed. A sign isn't the reality; it points to the reality. It's something that is visible and points to something that is currently

---

[41] Some suggest that these clouds of rising smoke compare with the cloud that hid Jesus from his disciples' sight upon his ascension (Ac. 1:9-11). In a similar manner, Jesus' coming here was hidden from sight. This is one possible way of interpreting the invisible nature of this coming. Interestingly, Josephus, Eusebius, and the *Talmud* record that angelic armies were visibly seen in the clouds just before Jerusalem's destruction. This also could be interpreted as "the sign of his coming," since Jesus is the commander of the heavenly hosts.

invisible. The fall of Jerusalem was the sign that announced the final "last days" of the Jewish age, not the Christian or Church age, to which there is no end. These days were still the *beginning days* of the Christian age.

Thus, Jesus' predictions were all fulfilled. This should be perfectly clear, unless we're looking through a futurist veil. There is no need to explain away anything or do a fancy dance around any scripture. Nor should we be surprised that God chose to send Christ in judgment to destroy Jerusalem in A.D. 70 in the same way He had come out of heaven many times before in Old Covenant times "with myriads of holy ones" (Dt. 33:2). Jesus, who had come, died, arose, and gone back to heaven, came out of heaven to judge the very people upon whom He had spoken seven woes (Mt. 23). The time of grace upon the Jewish nation had elapsed (Mt. 27:25; 2Th. 1:7-8; Jude 14; Ro. 11:26; Isa. 59: 20-21; 27:9). It's a fact of biblical and redemptive history.

In all this, Jesus' prophetic words, the imminency statements of every New Testament writer, and the expectations of the early Church can be plainly understood, in our day, as true and inspired. Yet no one except God the Father knew the final day or hour (exact time) of this "time of the end" (Da. 12:7). Nor can we look back today and reconstruct or know for certain when the literal last day or final hour was. The exact day or hour is not important, but the destruction of biblical Judaism is highly important. It was prophesied; it was fulfilled.

Thus, Jesus' predictions were all fulfilled. This should be perfectly clear, unless we're looking through a futurist veil.

Chapter 11

Why Does It Really Matter?

The issues of eschatology are not trivial pursues of irrelevant matters. According to R.C. Sproul, "It has been argued that no less than two thirds of the content of the New Testament is concerned directly or indirectly with eschatology."[42] Other scholars have estimated that 25 to 30 percent of the whole Bible is so concerned.

So we are not dealing with a fringe issue. One's particular view, non-view, or confusion over the fulfillment of end-time Bible prophecy will greatly impact one's understanding, or lack of understand, of many other significant things the Bible teaches, as well. Such as:

- the nature of your salvation, presently
- the relevance of the kingdom of God in your life, here and now
- what happens to a believer immediately after physical death
- much more!

Think of eschatology this way. It is more than "the study of last things," as it's usually defined. It's the study of what Christ

[42] R.C. Sproul, "A Journey Back in Time," *Tabletalk Magazine,* January 1999, 5.

has or has not yet done for us and a very important part of God's revelation to we humans. That's why two thirds of the New Testament is so concerned!

Indeed, a correct view of the fulfillment of end-time Bible prophecy really does matter. As we've seen, the liberals and skeptics have hit Christianity at its two weakest points: (1) Jesus' time-restricted promises to return within the lifetime of his first hearers. (2) The imminency expectations of every New Testament writer and the early Church. And "hope deferred" has made the Church "sick" (Pr. 13:12)—in many ways!

Hopefully, this book has opened your eyes. Something is severely wrong with the way Christianity, in general, has attempted to circumvent the challenge of informed critics and skeptics. Not being willing to admit that the inspired writers of Scripture and even Jesus were mistaken, we've come up with a variety of side-stepping devices and literary gymnastics to try and get around the plain, literal meaning of "embarrassing" words and statements. As a result, we have not only failed to counter our opponents' assaults, but we have developed a confusing and divisive eschatological system in the process. It's a house built on sand, because it is rooted in the traditions of men, and not on the Word of God. It insists on unscriptural delay and postponement and thereby greatly nullifies the Word of God and makes it of "none effect." (Mk. 7:13; Mt. 15:6 – NIV-KJV).

Preterism, on the other hand, is the only approach to eschatology that respects the time indicators. It takes seriously what the Bible says about "when." Therefore, the preterist can defend the integrity and inspiration of the whole Bible in the face of the liberal/skeptic attack. We argue that the time statements are not elastic, but mean what they say. They must be honored and taken at their normal, literal, plain, face-value meaning just as their original audience did. This means that we must spot the unscriptural manipulations and explaining-away tactics of so many interpreters. Nothing was postponed. Nothing was delayed.

Everything has been fulfilled right on time in its divinely ordained, 1st-century time context. This is why the New Testament writers were talking the way they did and with such certainty. It's the most natural reading and understanding of the texts.

One other point we cannot overemphasize in conclusion, is that scholars from many different perspectives confirm that the Apostle Paul, Peter, John, the writer of Hebrews and their contemporaries expected "the end" and the soon fulfillment of "all things" in their lifetime. They understood the eschatological language as applying personally to them and with urgent significance. Let's also never forget that they were being guided by the Holy Spirit into all truth and shown the things to come (Jn. 16:13). Apparently, what they expected was what the Holy Spirit showed them. And no New Testament writer ever corrected that understanding. Consequently, their expectations did not prove false. The Spirit of truth did not become the Spirit of falsehood (1Jn 4:6; 5:6). Everything makes perfect sense if we leave the time of fulfillment it in its proper historical context and begin adjusting our understanding of its nature—not vice versa which is what we have been doing incorrectly for the past 19 centuries and counting.

On the other hand, if history has proven that the New Testament writers' expectations were wrong on such a monumental issue as this, how can we trust them to have conveyed other aspects of the faith to us correctly? The honest and sincere answer to this question is why Preterism continues to grow steadily among conservative, evangelical believers. After all, isn't it just like God to have worked out everything, perfectly and harmoniously, no gaps, no gimmicks, no interruptions, and no weaknesses for which we have to make up excuses or devise desperate postponement charades to cover up? Our critics don't buy it. Neither should we.

If history has proven that the New Testament writers' expectations were wrong on such a monumental issue as this, how can we trust them to have conveyed other aspects of the faith to us correctly?

Conclusion

Will You Join Us?

The *only* effective response to the liberal/skeptic attack on the Bible and on the credibility and divinity of Jesus Christ is not more side-stepping devices or literary gymnastics. The *only* *solution* to the problem of non-occurrence is OCCURRENCE. Only the preterist view offers this solution. That solution, as Proverbs 13:12b states, is "but a longing fulfilled is a tree of life."

Preterists confirm that everything Jesus promised was fulfilled exactly *as* and *when* He said it would, and exactly *as* and *when* every New Testament writer expected as they were guided by the Holy Spirit into all truth and shown the things to come (Jn. 16:13). This fulfillment realization is truly "a tree of life." It is also the most Christ-honoring, Scripture-authenticating, and faith-validating of all the end-time positions in the historic Church. What's more, it will provide a solid biblical understanding and appreciation of the nature of Christ's finished work on our behalf.

So when the turn of millennium comes and goes and nothing of any eschatological significance comes to pass (and it won't), the Preterist position stands poised with better answers, better explanations, a better hope, and a better worldview for all Christians (see Appendices A & B). For non-Christians, it offers the most compelling argument for looking into the claims of Christianity. Why can we make these statements with such assurance? It's because, brothers and sister, "the end" the Bible proclaims is behind us, not ahead of us. The "last days" are past, not present or future (Heb. 1:2). The Bible's one-and-only "end" was covenantal, not cosmic. It was the end of the age of Moses, not the Christian age. And Jesus did return, bodily and literally, just *as* and *when* He said He would. He no longer is departed. He is here with us! It's all part of our faith which "was once for all delivered [past tense] to the saints" [literally] (Jude 3).[43]

That faith wasn't *partially* delivered with the rest delayed or put on hold. More is not yet-to-be-delivered. It was "once for all delivered" within consistent and biblically defined time parameters that Scripture imposed upon itself. Sadly, this completed faith is greatly un- and under-realized, primarily due to postponement and abandonment eschatology. Thankfully, this is changing.

So will you join with us in this next Reformation and Renewal of Christianity—the Prophecy Reformation? As has been true in previous times, some will be reformers. Some will be resisters. And some will be opponents. As usual, the choice is yours.

The *only solution* to the problem of nonoccurrence is OCCURRENCE.

---

[43] For more on Jesus' invisible bodily return —see presenter's book, *Beyond the End Times*, 195-202.

Publisher's Postscript

Four Classic Objections

Since the presentation and re-naming of John Noē's original ETS paper titled, *The Only Solution to the Liberal/Skeptic Attack on the Bible*, we received a few objections from fellow conservative Christians expressing concern with our approach. Here are four of those objections, along with my responses, and a retold version of the classic "David and Goliath" story.

Objection #1 –

"I don't care for the *Dead In Their Tracks* title at all. It's too bombastic, too braggadocios, and too personal. Do you really want to convey the message that you want liberals dead? In my experience, it is possible to have a winning, persuasive message without inflicting blunt force trauma on the recipient. Understatement is almost always better than overstatement, especially in the highly charged debate of the type in which you are engaged."

Publisher's Response –

First, the expression "dead in their tracks" does not mean killing people, but rather bringing their attack on the Bible to a dead stop. We certainly should not overstate our case, but many of us believe the conservative church needs some "blunt force trauma" to wake it up out of its "escapist, retreatist, defeatist, withdrawal" mindset. The conservative evangelical church has lost much ground in the culture war and in the "battle for the Bible." Liberals have taken control of most of the oldest and largest seminaries in this country. At meetings of the Evangelical Theological Society, conservatives are wringing their hands and whining about the need for an effective counterattack, yet none has been forthcoming.

Only the preterist view has the solution to this problem that the liberals used to get their foot in the door. It is way past time for us to counterattack, especially now that we have a real solution. We can "answer them convincingly," as R.C. Sproul has challenged us to do. It is criminal to have the antidote to liberal poison and not let the victims know it is available. And, it is suicide to know the antidote is available and refuse to believe in it and make use of it.

Our tradition-bound "big brothers" have a hard time believing there is a solution, so they have allowed liberal Goliaths to taunt and ridicule with impunity. But our young, bright theological students (the little Davids) will discover their weak spot, stop them "dead in their tracks," and take the turf back from the liberals the same way the liberals snatched in from us (one young bright seminary student at a time). They will become the leaders in those seminaries and reverse the liberal policies. This may take a few generations to accomplish (like the first Reformation did), but it has to start somewhere, and books like this can make it happen. Ideas have consequences.

This book's bold title and cover art was specifically designed to be a wake-up call to the whole theological community, and to alert the next generation of conservative theologians that a real solution has finally arrived. They are still untainted by the liberals and daring enough to seize a good solution when they find it. This book has what they are looking for—the right stuff to stop the liberal attack.

John Noē has dedicated himself to being a spark that will help ignite the next big shockwave of reform—a reformation so powerful that I believe it will dwarf the previous one in its multi-generational impact and worldview change. I share that vision and passion. Preterists are not playing games. This is world-changing stuff. We are calling for "reformation" of the "prophecy" views of the church. We want to change the worldview of the church so she can change the world's view of Christ.

This is not a time to be politically correct, pleasantly insipid, and impotent as doves. We need to be men of God who will tell it the way it really is, like David did when he told Goliath what he was about to do to him "in the name of the Lord of Hosts" (1 Sam. 17:45-47):

> This day the Lord will deliver you up into my hands, and I will strike you down and remove your head from you. And I will give the dead bodies of the army of the Philistines this day to the birds of the sky and wild beasts of the earth, that all the earth may know that there is a God in Israel.

With the Lord's help, David made good on that boast. And the preterist view can substantiate its claim to be the "only solution" that can stop the liberal attack "dead in their tracks." They were the first to take it personal with their attack on Jesus and the inspired New Testament writers. As little David said of Goliath, "this uncircumcised Philistine ... has taunted the armies of the Living God." These liberals (uncircumcised of heart) have mocked God's only begotten Son and vilified His Holy Word. Attacks like this deserve His "blunt force trauma." Proverbs 26:3 says, "A whip is for the horse, a bridle for the donkey, and a rod for the back of fools." Goliath got what he was asking for. And God will not spare the rod on the liberal backside. They deserve to be exposed, refuted, and repulsed to the "full extent of the law of Christ."

It is time we proclaimed "the only solution" from the rooftops of the temples of modern culture. May the Lord God Almighty raise up a huge army of little Davids to heap shame on the liberal/skeptic Goliaths who have raised themselves up against Christ and His Word. The most unlikely little Davids will be used by God, so that "all will know that the Lord does not deliver by sword or by spear, for the battle is the Lord's and He will give [the liberal] into our hands." (1 Sam. 17:47). And God gets all the credit, since only He can accomplish something like that.

May this book be a little stone that God guides into the forehead of the liberal/skeptic establishment to bring it crashing down into disrepute, so that God's Word will stand tall and vindicated, and we be able to hear those beautiful words, "Well done...."

Objection #2 –

"I do not think that our job is to prove the critics wrong, nor is it to close the cracks of our theology so that they cannot get in. The critics will be critics till Jesus changes their hearts. My answer to the problem is 'already, not yet.' I believe that some prophecy has partial fulfillment now and complete fulfillment later. Dual fulfillment seems to be another solution. It has to be an option for me since I believe that there were times when Jesus spoke in words that were hard to understand and I believe he will yet return."

Publisher's Response –

This is the kind of wimpy under-reaction I have seen time after time. I just don't think this person has his head in the game. He doesn't realize what is at stake here—the authority of Jesus and the Bible. As long as the liberals and skeptics were weak and scarce, the church could get away with wimpy responses like this. But things have changed. As Sproul says, we have no choice now but to "answer them convincingly." I'm tired of seeing the "giant" win and our conservative big brothers telling us to go back to the sheepfold! It is time for a few Goliaths to hit the dust.

Fact is, conservatives know they have no solution to the problem, so they don't even try. But they don't believe the liberal is correct either, so they try to ignore him hoping he will fizzle out and vanish. They seem to think that since they don't have a solution, there must not be a real problem. It is sheer denial of reality. But the liberals aren't vanishing. They are growing stronger and more entrenched by the day.

This is why this book is so important. It shows that there really is a serious problem and that Preterism has the only solution. Already, too many conservative scholars have walked into the enemy's camp and laid their armor down, theologically as well as culturally. Let's face it, we live in a world where the concept of absolute truth is under fire and postmodern ideas sweep across the cultural landscape like a storm wind. Preterism has the solution to the culture war also. Inaction, silence, abandonment theology, retreatism, defeatism, short-term thinking, and escapism has not and cannot win. No other worldview can succeed against these forces of humanism and anti-God/anti-Christianity like the long-term, optimistic, get-involved worldview generated by Preterism. This book does more than just suggest abstract theological ideas. It outlines a solid biblical theology and a vibrant worldview.

Objection #3 –

"The early-church fathers (post A.D. 70) did not recognize that Jesus returned in A.D. 70. So neither will I."

Publisher's Response –

This is like the Bereans saying, "The rabbis do not recognize Jesus as Messiah, so neither will we." It's the blind following the blind. The lack of recognition by the early church is certainly surprising, but not insurmountable nor inexplicable. But it poses a real dilemma for conservative Christians. Which would you rather believe? That Jesus and the apostles were mistaken, or that the early church misunderstood and misinterpreted the *time* and *nature* of fulfillment? This is exactly the problem we face. Why are we so quick to defend the integrity of the creeds and uninspired churchmen, while leaving the inspiration of Christ and the apostles defenseless? This is "invalidating the Word of God for the sake of your tradition" (Mk. 7:13), just like the Pharisees did with their rabbinical traditions.

A mistake has to be charged to either Jesus and the inspired New Testament writers, or to the uninspired church fathers. Liberals and skeptics have left us no alternative. One of the two groups was in error. We cannot preserve the integrity of both. I do not hesitate in laying the accusation at the feet of the uninspired church fathers, since the only alternative is to strip Christ and the apostles of their inspiration and integrity, as the liberals and skeptics have done.

Christians need to face the fact that we have erred on this matter. The C. S. Lewis quote in the first chapter of this book provides a pathetic example. Lewis believed Jesus was mistaken. He leaves Christ in the jaws of the skeptic. If this ruffles some conservative feathers, then some feathers need to be ruffled. Again, the liberals are capturing more turf by the day. It is time we fought back with something of substance to solve the problem rather than add to it. It's time for the next generation of young conservative evangelicals to rise up and use the powerful apologetic weaponry of the preterist view to take back the turf we have lost to the liberals and the skeptics. Will you join us?

Objection #4 –

"You should avoid such phrases as "the only possible solution." It seems extremely arrogant for anyone to claim such a thing. Modesty would be much more appropriate. When you say there is only one possible solution, this implies that every other one, including ones not even thought up yet, are wrong. This sort of reason, in some contexts, is legitimate, but in general in the context or environment of theories it is not legitimate. I would be very careful about this sort of language or reason."

Publisher's Response –

How long is "long enough" for us to wait for another "possible solution" to the liberal/skeptic attack to surface? The conservative evangelical world has had 1900 years to come up with a solution, and they have failed. If I believed for a second that the preterist view is *not* the only possible solution, I would be happy to soften or abandon this terminology. But there is no other possible solution to "non-occurrence" than "occurrence." Either it occurred, or Jesus is a false prophet. Liberals and skeptics have already tested and rejected all the other "artful dodges" that conservatives have proposed. Partial fulfillment and multiple fulfillments just won't cut it. Nothing counters "non-fulfillment" like "fulfillment." As John Noë says in this book, "the only solution to non-occurrence is occurrence." This is the only "theory" they can't get around. You can't get any better than that.

Sure, the liberal "Goliaths" will howl in scorn, and our evangelical "big brothers" will advise us to use their "tried, traditional" armor. But the next generation of scholars will see the power of the "occurrence" idea. Liberals depend on recruiting the youngest and brightest to their cause. When those youngsters start not only staying in the conservative camp, but actually attacking the liberals and winning back some of their brightest scholars, the

Philistines will retreat! And our "big brothers" will pat us on the back and join us in pursuing the Philistines to plunder them.

We cannot back off this "only solution" and "dead in their tracks" approach. We are the only ones who have this huge advantage. It is the very thing that will attract the best and brightest young scholars to the conservative cause. It is the finest apologetic weapon the conservative cause has ever had. Press the battle with it. Don't back off just because our "big brothers" have queasy stomachs! Let them stay down in the valley (and live "lives of quiet desperation" – Thoreau) at the foot of the mountain where it is "safe." We need to "attack the mountain." It is the very thing that will attract the best and brightest young scholars to the conservative cause.

Perhaps some of John Noē's mountain-climbing slogans from his first book, *Peak Performance Principles for High Achievers*, would apply here?

"It takes less energy to go for the top than to wallow in the valley of frustration and anguish!"

"People will try to hold you back . . . to conform!"

"We make many little choices that either lead us ever upward or lead us along the path of mediocrity!"

"The great rewards of life come to those with the heart to persist and the courage to step away from the pessimistic crowd!"

"Set God-sized goals!"

Preterists have the "only solution" to the Goliath dilemma that liberalism and skepticism have forged against Christ. I urge all conservatives who believe in the inerrancy and absolute authority of Scripture to join us in this reformation effort.

The Story of David and Goliath Retold

Long ago, a sheep farmer named Jesse sent his youngest son David with food to visit his big brothers who were on the front lines battling the Philistines. When David arrived, a giant named Goliath was out front taunting the army of Israel and mocking their God. Young David couldn't believe the Israelites were just standing there, while this uncircumcised Philistine blasphemed and mocked.

The giant represents the liberal/skeptic establishment, wielding a powerful destructive influence with their "non-fulfillment" arguments. Little David represents the Preterist with his "fulfillment" slingshot.

David cried out, "If you are not going to fight him, I will." His big brothers remarked, "With what great theological weapons and armor are you going to fight him? Your little preterist slingshot? Get back to your sheep, you little heretic!"

David takes out his little preterist slingshot, and says, "Nope, I won't go home until this giant falls. You guys obviously don't have any weapons strong enough to stop him. You cannot defeat non-fulfillment giants with mere partial fulfillment armor. My preterist slingshot may not look like much, but it can do something traditional arguments cannot do! It can counter the liberal in the place where he is most vulnerable—his heady "non-fulfillment" arguments.

So, David took his little preterist slingshot and approached the giant. Again, Goliath ridiculed the integrity of Christ and Scripture and anyone "stupid enough to believe in it." David's big brothers looked on in horror. At first they wanted to pretend they were not similar to him in any way, and then they wondered what they would tell their dad about little David being fed to the birds after Goliath made minced meat out of his arguments.

But David is too consumed by godly indignation over the giant's blasphemy to be worried about any of those things. And he knew he had a solution to the giant liberal/skeptic problem. So, he looks the giant in the eyes and says, "This day I will strike your non-fulfillment arguments down and remove them from the theological playing field and display their dead carcasses openly as the trophies of conservatism. Then all the world will know that there is an answer to your attack on Christ and His Word."

Goliath made his move. David ran right at him and slung his stone and struck the giant on the forehead—his place of greatest vulnerability. Goliath fell on his face. David had no sword, so he used Goliath's own form-text criticism to finish him off.

Now comes the part I've been building up to. Notice what happens next. When the giant's army of liberals and skeptics saw that their champion was dead, they fled, and the men of Israel pursued them and converted many back to the conservative cause. They also put the preterist view into their seminary curriculum to insure that many more of their young warriors would never be infected by those liberal arguments again.

Lastly, something even more interesting happened. David's big brothers quit criticizing and started to buddy up to little brother David. They no longer wanted to send him back to the sheep. He was a valuable asset now. Let him inspire the troops. And get him in the seminary lecture circuit, training the young soldiers how to kill liberal giants.

There are several morals to this "retold" story. The first is that big-headed liberals need to watch out for little preterist stones flying in the air. A second is that David's big brothers need to pay closer attention to what their little brother is doing and how he is doing it. The third is that we little Davids need to speak tenderly to our big brothers in the conservative evangelical camp and not burn the bridges. We need to take them food to strengthen them in their fight against the liberals and skeptics. And while we're at it, show them the only real solution to the liberal/skeptic attack.

I long for the day when we will see thousands of bright young theological students flocking to conservative seminaries again, but this time to learn how to use preterist slingshots, rather than seeing them become liberals and skeptics by default. That's my vision. Come kill a few giants with us!

Edward E. Stevens
Publisher & President
International Preterist Association

Appendix A

Your Worldview

What you believe shapes your actions. Your view of the timing for the fulfillment of end-time prophecy will significantly affect your worldview—i.e., your outlook for the future, your conduct in the present, and your motivation for being an ambassador in Christ's kingdom on earth, here and now.

If you expect the world (or state of things) to get worse and worse until the Lord comes back very soon to rapture you out, that will affect your worldview. It also takes much of the significance out of human action and plays right into the hands to those who are hostile to Christianity. They are more than willing to rush in and fill the vacuum created by your withdrawal. All of which is just interpreted as just another sign of the end by many futurists.

Let's face it, if you believe this world is soon going to be destroyed, your motivation for thinking long-term and committing to efforts that will make it a better place for future generations will be noticeably affected. After all, "why bother?" This is a far-too-prevailing Christian attitude of our time. In the words of the old saying, "Why polish brass on a sinking ship?" But it's a natural response for those conditioned to the termination/futuristic/"Left Behind" message that is so popular.

On the other hand, your motivation is going to be quite different if you believe Jesus has already returned *as* and *when* He said He would, and that He has consummated his kingdom and expects you to reign with Him on earth, here and now (Rev. 5:9-10). Essentially, that's the difference between the worldview of Preterism and that of Premillennialism. In the popular Premillennial worldview, one strives to hang on until the end. But in the Preterist worldview, one has compelling, positive reasons to undertake dynamic roles in the present, both individually and corporately, to build a better future and to benefit succeeding generations. Big difference! Huge difference!

Fact is, most evangelicals have been conditioned to wait for a future 1,000 period before they begin to reign with Christ. They've been taught that when the Jews crucified Jesus the kingdom He came and died to bring was postponed. If that's right, somebody, or the Holy Spirit, forgot to clue in the Apostle Paul. Twenty to thirty years after this supposed postponement event, Paul is running around the Roman Empire preaching and teaching "the kingdom of God and . . . the Lord Jesus Christ" (Ac. 28:31; 19:8, 20). Didn't he know it had been postponed?

No wonder, with this as the prevailing view, that the Church's influence here in America has severely waned in just this century. But if the world is not going to end, if the ship is not sinking, if we will not be taken out of this world (in accordance with Jesus' prayer for all believers [Jn. 14:15, 20]), we need to be about our Father's business—and that is, reigning with Christ on earth and expanding his kingdom (Rev. 5:9-10; 20:4-5; 22:1-5; Jn. 14:12)!

Make no mistake, ideas have consequences! And what we believe, eschatologically, affects what we will or won't do. The popular but unbiblical idea that we are now living in the "last days" and that Jesus very soon coming back to rescue us out of this world and its troubles has been and still is highly detrimental to the cause of Christ, the effectiveness of his Church, and the willingness of Christians to be salt and light, here and now.

Ever since the middle part of this century when the premillennial dispensational view displaced the postmillennial view as the dominant eschatological position, this has perfectly coincided with the abandonment of many Christians from involvement in our society and the decline of the Church as the moral influence. In retrospect, we Christians here in America have managed to give away, in the last 50 to 60 years or so, most of the institutions our Christian ancestors established—the government, the schools, the universities—and all without much of a fight. Actually, it was a unilateral withdrawal. How did this happen? A flawed worldview! The termination eschatology espoused by the vast majority of evangelicals today is at the root of this abandonment and retreat psychology.

John W. Chalfant, the author of the book, *Abandonment Theology,* concurs:

> . . . much of the clergy, along with their millions of victimized American Christians following their pastors' lead, have retreated from the battlefront to the social, non-confrontational, non-controversial reservation. They say that Christians should confine their religious activities to politically non-controversial roles and keep their Bibles out of the political process. They also say that based on prophecy these are the 'last days,' and any efforts we make to restore righteousness to this nation will be in vain and need not even be undertaken.[44]

What a vastly different worldview the preterist view gives us about both the past and the future. This change from a postponement perspective to a fulfilled perspective offers believers a different dynamic for Christian witness and involvement in our world. Edward E.Stevens, President of the International Preterist Association says it well:

---

[44] John W. Chalfant, *Abandonment Theology* (Winter Park, FL: America – A Call to Greatness, 1996), 117-118.

This [Preterist] view offers a much more positive and realistic worldview. It is conservative, consistent, optimistic, responsible and accountable. And it robs us of no motivation for either living the Christian life, or evangelizing the world. In fact, it's the only view which gives us a consistent reason for being constructively involved in making our world a better place for the long-term, unlike the short-term escapist and withdrawal mindset of most futurists.[45]

So why is a proper understanding about the end times important for you and the Church? Because eschatological ideas have worldview consequences. And Christianity has been ill-served by the postponing futurist views. Nor does eschatology need to be confusing, mysterious or divisive, as it has become. Indeed, we have been overlooking something very simple. Edward E. Stevens further writes:

The 'problem of imminency,' continually hurled at us by the skeptics, still remains in regard to the Parousia, Resurrection, and Judgment. Only the fully consistent Preterist view has been able to stop their [liberal/skeptic] assault dead in its tracks. Sure, our answer challenges the creeds, but it 'handles accurately the Word of God' and 'takes every [skeptical] thought captive,' reforms the weak and impotent eschatology that we have been saddled with for the past 20 centuries, and generates the only really long-term victorious worldview that can carry us through the rest of eternity. That is more than enough reason for any conservative Bible believer to take a look at it.[46]

Amen! Now are you willing to take a good look?

---

[45] Edward E. Stevens, "What Is The Preterist View of Bible Prophecy" flyer (Bradford, PA: International Preterist Association, accessed 21 March 2000); available from http://www.preterist.org/resources/aboutpreterism.htm; Internet.
[46] Edward E. Stevens, *Questions About The Afterlife* (Bradford, PA: International Preterist Association, 1999), 50.

**Make no mistake, ideas have
consequences!**

Appendix B

Futurism—An Eschatology of Despair

by James D. Craig, Ph.D.

The following unpublished article was written at my request by an associate minister of a large independent Christian church here in Indianapolis, Indiana. Jim is a godly man, a wise counselor, and has been a partial preterist since 1974. I've decided to include it as an appendix in this book for reasons that will become obvious as you read it.

John Noē

Late in 1999, I logged-on to one of the many web sites featuring futurist Bible prophecy. The message was predictable: earthquakes, crime, and war prove the End is near; the Antichrist is already alive, and is about to appear; the Rapture and the Great Tribulation are right around the corner.

The site also featured a "Letters" section, allowing listeners to post comments and questions. One lady initiated a discussion by reporting:

> I would like to know if anyone else is experiencing the conflict between the everyday worldly routine and the impending Rapture. So much of what I am expected to do on a daily basis (my basic responsibilities) seem meaningless in light of Jesus' imminent return. I find it difficult to concentrate on the mundane things when there is so much going on in terms of prophecy playing out in front of me. I feel that God expects me to continue to fulfill my responsibilities as an employee, a mother, a neighbor, etc., since He told us to occupy until He returned, but it is increasingly difficult for me to focus on things that won't exist much longer.

Other readers posted similar thoughts and feelings. For example, a 55 year-old grandmother wrote:

> I too struggle with my feeling that the time is so short that nothing else I do is important. Shopping, feeding and caring for my chickens and dogs and cats, gardening, and so on seems like it is a waste of time as I see more and more clearly that the organized church is sliding down hill. I keep wondering how much worse it can get and yet it keeps getting worse. I still struggle with how far we are to go as far as not voting or anything. I haven't voted lately but what about issues involving bans on partial birth abortions? I am probably fretting about nothing as all this is usually up to Congress anyway and not us.

A discouraged pastor wrote:

> I used to be so vigilant about emailing my senator, etc. But I have come to think, after reading (futurist literature) that a much bigger agenda is at work.

Another believer wrote:

> I have always felt that it was my responsibility to be active politically. Now, however, I have a new perspective. I see where my political activism on behalf of the religious right was really a

statement to the world that THIS is my home, when in fact I am just passing through. I am truly in shock. I feel as though I have been working for the enemy.

These letters illustrate the everyday impact of futurist teaching. Most followers will not quit their jobs, cash out, move to Israel, and wait for the Rapture. Rather, they will fulfill daily responsibilities but find these tasks to be meaningless; obey the law, but see little point in working to elect pro-life candidates; join a church, but support it half-heartedly.

In response to these despairing notes, the futurist pastor operating the web page offered this instruction:

> As Christians, we have to obey the Lord's leading. If we feel we should vote, we vote. That is an individual matter. When it comes to issues such as abortion, we have to stand again with the Lord and His Word. The question is, do we do anything about it? Again, it depends on how the Lord leads you. We don't condone it, but whether we should march or not is an individual decision.
>
> The real issue is our orientation—earthly or heavenly. We are salt and light to the world because of our fresh and living relationship with Jesus Christ that shines through us. But we are citizens of a heavenly kingdom, a city whose builder and maker is God. This is Satan's world and ultimately we are not going to change or reform it. We are here to snatch people out of this kingdom of darkness and into the kingdom of light.

In other words, this futurist instructs Christians to follow God's leading by following their feelings. He seems to understand that the Bible decries abortion, but believes God may lead people to do nothing about it. He knows Christians are salt and light, but believes they cannot preserve and guide a nation. He reasons that staying home on Election Day is an acceptable option because

Christians have no power to change a world owned by Satan. He concludes that escape is the only hope.

(We should be thankful America's armed forces did not adopt these views in the 20th Century! In my opinion, it is shameful to offer Memorial Day honors to those who died for our freedom and then say the world they fought to liberate belongs to Satan.)

The pastor's sentiments explain why some futurists silently cheer when thousands die in an earthquake, drought triggers widespread starvation, homosexual activists win a case before the Supreme Court, or an Arab state launches missiles at Israel. Their eschatology creates a hunger and thirst for unrighteousness and a mandate to rejoice in evil. With eyes fixed on a "blessed hope" of imminent escape, futurist leaders steadfastly refuse to see the depressing, paradoxical consequences their teachings produce in so many of their followers.

Faulty Information

For over nineteen centuries, futurists have been miscalculating the time of Christ's return, proclaiming various world leaders to be the Antichrist; and misleading people to make decisions based on the idea that the Great Tribulation is soon to occur. As a result, millions of outspoken Christians have gone to their graves absolutely convinced they would live to see the Second Coming. In doing so, they forfeited their credibility, made poor personal and financial decisions, left a legacy of ignorance and gullibility, and unwittingly discredited the Gospel message.

Several years ago, I saw a commercial for a futurist video designed to rescue unfortunate souls who will be caught in the Great Tribulation. The ad depicted a Christian housewife trying desperately to get her beer-guzzling husband to accept Christ and escape the coming holocaust. As he ignored her and continued watching the ballgame on TV, she waved a videotape and said "Soon, I'll be gone in the Rapture, and the Great Tribulation will begin. But I'm leaving this video that explains how you can be saved. I'm putting it right here in this drawer." The ad then told viewers how to get their own copy of the videotape, major credit cards accepted.

Where are those tapes today? Some are still in drawers gathering dust. Others have found their way to the local landfill. All give silent testimony to the fallacies of futurism and rich comedic material for those who mock Christianity.

What Millions of Christians Want to Hear

Given such outcomes, why do millions of Christians continue to invest so much money in end times books, seminars, and tapes? The answer is simple: They are buying what they want to hear.

Conservative Christians believe the Scriptures are truthful and relevant, and they listen to those who support these views. Futurists assure them that the Scriptures accurately predict present day and future events, then bury them in a blizzard of Bible verses taken out of context. Futurists claim to take the Bible literally, and accuse their critics of making the Bible say something other than what it plainly means. Lacking the technical Bible study tools, knowledge of history, or time to sort through these contentions, conservative Christians conclude that futurism is the only position available to the Bible-believer.

A minority of Christians is drawn to futurism for another reason. They have abdicated their role of salt and light in this sin-sick world. They welcome messages that justify their cultural silence and withdrawal. Affluent, morally compromised, immersed in the cares of this world, and unwilling to bear the costs associated with rebuilding a Christian culture, they pay teachers to absolve them of their culpability and assure them that their children and grandchildren will not have to bear the consequences.

These Christians want to hear that the current cultural decline has been prophesied in the Scriptures, and that any attempt to stop it is futile and perhaps a violation of God's will. So what if Social Security goes broke in 2020 and the elderly have no money to buy food or medicine? So what if a liberal President appoints pro-abortion judges who legalize the stripping of newborn infants for replacement parts? So what if the public schools become detention camps or the streets become war zones? The very people who should care most about these things—Bible-believing Christians—are paying futurist writers and teachers to tell them that they will be long gone before these problems can affect them personally.

Conclusion

We all know futurists who are not gloom-and-doom types. That is, we all know futurists who act as if their eschatology is not true. Almost 25 years ago, a famous futurist hired a landscape architect to draw up plans for his new campus. Oak seedlings were selected to frame the driveway—trees would need at least twenty years to resemble those on the color rendering presented to the ministry's Board of Trustees. At the same time this relatively long-term project was going on outside, the ministry inside was broadcasting programs warning that the world would end sometime in the late 1980s.

Futurists do build schools, crisis pregnancy centers, universities, and other long-term institutions. But to do so, they must first set aside their eschatology—or at least spin it in a manner that defies logic. It is my hope that Christians will notice this glaring inconsistency and begin exploring a compelling alternative—the historic preterist view.

According to this view, Christ did predict the End, provide discernable signs of the times, and instruct His followers to be watchful. The End came just as Christ predicted in AD 70 as the armies of Rome trampled the city of Jerusalem, slaughtered its citizens, and utterly destroyed the Temple. Thanks to Jesus' early warning system, the Church survived the Great Tribulation, became the New Jerusalem, and inherited the identity, promises, and blessings of God's chosen people.

The preterist view allows the text of Scripture to mean exactly what it says—that Christ would return in judgment within the lifetime of His contemporaries. It is grounded in accurate hermeneutics (the science of Bible interpretation) and supported by history. I recommend it for your careful consideration.

For more information, contact:

James D. Craig, Ph.D.
2631 Stanford Court
Indianapolis, IN 46268
e-mail: jcfishing@aol.com

WORKS CITED

Answering-Christianity.com. "The Ultimate Test of Jesus: Jesus' second coming and 'grace.'" Available from http://www.arabianebarzaar.com/ac/second.htm. Internet.

Chalfant, John W. *Abandonment Theology.* Winter Park, FL: America – A Call to Greatness, 1996.

Craig, James D. "Futurism—An Eschatology of Despair." Indianapolis, 2000. Unpublished article.

Gentry, Kenneth L. *He Shall Have Dominion.* Tyler, TX: Institute for Christian Economics, 1992.

Haddad, Yvonne Yazbeck and Wadi Z. Haddah, eds. *Christian-Muslim Encounters.* Gainesville: University Press of Florida, 1995.

Ice, Thomas. "Has Bible Prophecy Already Been Fulfilled? Part V." *Midnight Call Magazine*, October 1999, 22.

Ice, Thomas. "Has Bible Prophecy Already Been Fulfilled?" *Midnight Call Magazine*, June 1999, 23.

_____ and Kenneth L. Gentry. *The Great Tribulation Past or Future?* Grand Rapids: Kregel, 1999.

Kaplan, Aryeh. "Jesus and the Bible." In *The Real Messiah.* Reprinted from *Jewish Youth*, June 1973, Tammuz 5733, No. 40.

Kateregga, Badru D. *Islam and Christianity: A Muslim and a Christian in Dialogue*. Grand Rapids: Eerdmans, 1980, *re. ed* 1981.

Klausner, Joseph. *Jesus of Nazareth: His Life, Times, and Teaching*. New York: Macmillen, 1925.

Kung, Hans and Jurgen Moltmann, eds. *Islam: A Challenge for Christianity*. London: SCM Press, 1994.

Lazarus-Yafeh Hava. *Intertwined Worlds: Medieval Islam and Bible Criticism*. Princeton, NJ: Princeton University Press, 1992.

Levine, Samuel. *You Take Jesus, I'll Take God: How To Refute Christian Missionaries*. Los Angeles: Hamoroh Press, 1980.

Lewis, C.S. Essay "The World's Last Night" (1960). Found in *The Essential C.S. Lewis*. Lyle W. Dorsett, ed. New York: A Touchstone Book, Simon & Schuster, 1996.

Morey, Robert A. *The Islamic Invasion: Confronting the World's Fastest Growing Religion*. Eugene, Or.: Harvest House, 1992.

Noē, John. *Beyond the End Times: The Rest of...The Greatest Story Ever Told*. Bradford, PA: International Preterist Association, 1999.

_____ vs. Tommy Ice. "Preterist *vs.* Futurist" debate. Sponsored by Families Against Cults of Indiana, November 1999. Cassette.

Robinson, Neal. *Christ in Islam and Christianity*. Albany: State University of New York Press, 1991.

Russell, Bertrand. *Why I Am Not A Christian.* New York: A
Touchtone Book by Simon & Schuster, 1957.

Schweiterzer, Albert. *The Quest of the Historical Jesus.* New
York: The Macmillan Company, eighth printing, 1973.

Sproul, R.C. *The Last Days According to Jesus.* Grand Rapids:
Baker Books, 1998.

_____. "A Journey Back in Time." *Tabletalk Magazine,*
January 1999, 5.

_____. "Last Days Madness" presentation. Ligonier
Ministries' National Conference 1999. Cassette.

_____. "The Problem of Imminency" presentation, Covenant
Eschatology Symposium, Mt. Dora, FL. 1993. Cassette.

Stevens, Edward E. *Questions About The Afterlife.* Bradford, PA:
International Preterist Association, 1999.

_____. "What Is The Preterist View of Bible Prophecy" flyer.
Bradford, PA: International Preterist Association. Accessed 21
March 2000. Available from
http://www.preterist.org/resources/aboutpreterism.htm. Internet.

Stopler, Pinchas Stolper. "Was Jesus the Messiah Let's Examine
the Facts." In *The Real Messiah.* Rreprinted from *Jewish Youth,*
June 1973, Tammuz 5733, No. 40.

Zoba, Wendy Murry. "Islam, U.S.A.: Are Christians Prepared for
Muslims in the Mainstream?." *Christianity Today Magazize,* 3
April 2000, 40.

John Noe's books—and other preterist books and resources—are available from:

International Preterist Association
122 Seaward Ave, Bradford PA 16701-1515
1-888-257-7023 (orders only)

For more preterist information, contact us:
Ask for a free information packet, which includes
- An article, "What Is the Preterist View?"
- Sample issue of the preterist newsletter,
  The Preterist Link
- Book list and order form (about 50 books available)
- Tape list for audio and video

How to contact us:
- Phone: (814) 368-6578
- E-mail: preterist1@aol.com
- Web Site: http//preterist.org/resources

Browse our web site for preterist articles online—you can download and print. You can buy books and tapes using MC or Visa. You can ask questions and contact other preterists online.

International Preterist Association, Inc.
122 Seaward Avenue • Bradford PA 16701-1515 • USA

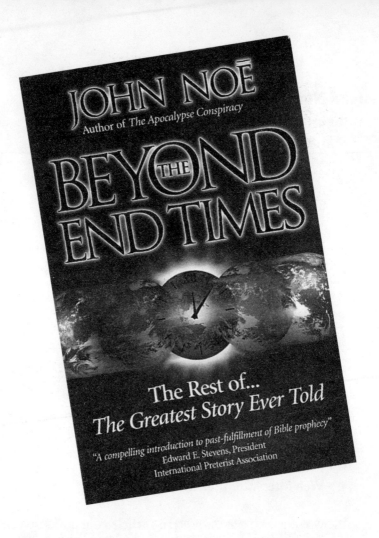

Beyond the End Times **Receives National Recognition!**

Christianity Today magazine has named John Noē's book as one of the top three to receive a Millennial Book Award recognition. *CT* Book Review Editor Mark Galli announces Noē's runner-up book with these words:

"In the and-now-for-something-a-little-different category, there is *Beyond the End Times: The Rest of the Greatest Story Every Told*, by John Noē (International Preterist Association, 314 pp., $19.95, paper).

Do We Really Need Another End-Times Book?

As long as the others fail to recognize that "the end" the Bible proclaims is behind us and not ahead of us, is past and not future, the answer is a resounding, YES! No consideration of the end times is complete without a look at the "past fulfillment" of prophecy. In this book you'll discover:

* WHY THE PERENNIAL PROPHETS OF DOOM HAVE BEEN AND ALWAYS WILL BE DEAD WRONG.
* WHY THE WORLD WILL NEVER-EVER END.
* HOW THE END FOR THE WORLD CAME RIGHT ON TIME.
* THE TIME AND NATURE OF CHRIST'S PAST RETURN.
* THE TRUE IDENTITY OF THE "NEW HEAVEN AND NEW EARTH."
* WHY THE FUTURE IS BRIGHT AND PROMISING.
* THE BASIS FOR THE NEXT REFORMATION OF CHRISTIANITY.

...While [others] debate the future Second Coming, John Noē argues that Jesus has *already* returned, as have the "last days" and "the judgment"—in the destruction of Jerusalem and the temple in A.D. 70. This view—preterism—has a small following, though the likes of R. C. Sproul admit to being at least a "partial preterist." Be that as it may, Noē, president of the Prophecy Reformation Institute, argues, with no little energy, against traditional views. He is finally unconvincing (at least to this amillennialist), but preterism does have an internal logic that makes for exegetically interesting reading."

Galli's article titled "The Millennial Book Awards" appeared in the October 25, 1999 issue of *Christianity Today*, pp 77–78.

What People Are Saying About John Noē's book *Beyond the End Times...*

Noē's book just could be the spark that ignites the next reformation of Christianity. – *James Earl Massey, Former Sr. Editor of Christianity Today and Dean Emeritus, School of Theology, Anderson University*

I predict this book will be a classic! – *John L. Bray, Evangelist*

John Noē has provided a fresh, open-minded look to the questions concerning the end times. His new work, *Beyond the End Times*, is a thoughtful and carefully reasoned interpretation of biblical prophecy. Many, like myself, will not be fully persuaded of his conclusions, but all will be challenged to read the biblical text more faithfully. Noe's work deserves very serious consideration. – *David S. Dockery, President of Union University, Jackson, TN*

This is an important work. You make an impressive case. One being made practically no where else in evangelical Christianity (to my knowledge) and one that deserves to be made and discussed... I can see this book attracting a lot of interest. – *Ronald J. Allen, Associate Professor, Christian Theological Seminary*

Your handling of Daniel's prophecies is revolutionary and needs as much exposure as it can get. – *Pastor Joe Lewis*

After reading *Beyond the End Times*, it was immediately apparent that this is the best popularly written book available in the field of fulfilled prophecy! Congratulations, John, on a great effort that will surely stand the test of time. – *Timothy R. King, President, Living Presence Ministries*

Your treatment of the "end of the world" is the best treatment of this idea that I had read that I can remember. Your book could really open the eyes of a lot of people. – *Walt Hibbard, Former Chairman, Great Christian Books*

The premise...is right on target... I am intensely interested in the unfolding of this approach. – *Knofel Staton, Past-President, Pacific Christian College*

What you are doing will shape the church for decades to come if not for centuries... Many people will be quoting you over the years to come.... – *Bruce Larson, Former Co-Pastor, The Crystal Cathedral, Adjunct Professor, Fuller Theological Seminary*

Your manuscript is interesting.... You have developed this theory in more detail than anyone else I know.... – *L. Russ Bush, Past-President, The Evangelical Theological Society*

It surely is a message that is desperately needed...So often, God has given his special gifts on understanding to lay people. John Calvin was a layman. John Noē is a layman. And both of them have left writings which the church must read and 'come to grips with.' – *Robert H. Schuller, The Crystal Cathedral*

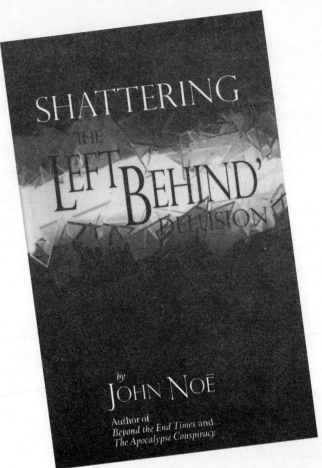

New Book
Shatters *'Left Behind'* Delusion

Award-Winning Author Offers Biblical Response to Popular End-Times Series

"Can books that have sold 18 million copies be wrong and their readers sadly deluded? Absolutely!" says John Noē.

The wildly popular *"Left Behind"* series of rapture books by Jerry Jenkins and Tim LaHaye is capturing massive popular attention. But we believe it is misleading millions in the process. John Noē is the first Christian leader to publicly describe the rapture theory they espouse as "tragically unbiblical."

Christians and non-Christians alike are being "caught up" in this new seductive teaching. They believe "the rapture" could occur at any moment. This book shatters that theory. Here's what this book covers:

More About "Shattering"

- *What the so-called Rapture is not*
- *How all "rapture" scriptures have been fulfilled*
- *What kind of resurrection body Christians get—and when*
- *What this means for Christians today and in the future*

Look for *Shattering the 'Left Behind' Delusion* at your local Christian bookstore, or purchase it direct from IPA for $12.95 (includes USA shipping and handling). Call your local Christian bookstore or IPA today and get your copy.

toll free: 1-888-257-7023 (USA only)
online: www.preterist.ORG/resources (VISA, Discover, MasterCard accepted)
email: Preterist1@aol.com
mail: International Preterist Assoc., 122 Seaward Ave., Bradford, PA 16701 USA

Prophecy Reformation Materials
by John Noē

(USA Postage Included)

Books:

Shattering the 'Left Behind' Delusion $12.95

*Beyond the End Times: The Rest of...The
Greatest Story Ever Told* $19.95

*Top Ten Misconceptions About Jesus'
Second Coming and the End Times* $6.00

Evangelical Theological Society Papers/Booklets:

Responsible Apocalypicism: What Is It and
How Do We Achieve It? $3.75

Israel: Popular Misconceptions About this Modern-
day Nation and Its Role in Bible Prophecy $3.75

Why We May Soon See the Return of
1st-Century Caliber Miracles and Effectiveness . . $3.75

The Many Comings of Jesus $3.75

Brochures:

12 Most Common Mistakes People Make
About Bible Prophecy and the End Times $1.00

The Solution to the Problem of the End Times . . $1.00

To order, send check or money order. For more information about John Noe's writing, speaking, and teaching
ministry, contact:

PRI
PROPHECY
REFORMATION
INSTITUTE

The Prophecy Reformation Institute
9715 Kincaid Drive Suite 1100
Fishers, IN 46038
Phone: (317) 841-7777
Fax: (317) 578-2110
Email: jnoe@prophecyrefi.org
Website: www.prophecyrefi.org

Notes

Notes

Notes

Notes

Notes

Notes